COOKING BOLD & FEARLESS

ILLUSTRATIONS BY HARRY DIAMOND

A Sunset Book

COOKING BOLD & FEARLESS

BY THE EDITORS OF SUNSET MAGAZINE
AND SUNSET BOOKS

Lane Books · Menlo Park, California

Third Printing March 1970

CONTENTS

...BECAUSE THEY LIKE TO EAT

Cooking bold and fearless is probably more typical of men than of women. Men cook mainly for pleasure and because they like to eat, rather than because they have to provide meals for the family 365 days out of the year. Also, since a male's stint in the kitchen is relatively short-lived, he feels freer to make the most of his time there. He isn't hesitant about striking off on new, untrodden paths of the culinary art; in addition to being fearless, he is adventurous.

This book consists of a collection of recipes that men have contributed to the Chefs of the West feature in *Sunset Magazine* over a ten-year period (though one goes all the way back to 1948, being a classic in its own right). Their contributions include family favorites, revived classics, and acquisitions from travel, as well as personal discoveries. Rather than being a carefully balanced group of recipes, this book presents simply the kinds of foods that men have enjoyed cooking.

Nevertheless, the men represented aren't one-shot "experts" whose range is limited to the frying pan, barbecue grill, salad bowl, or package mix. The breadth of talent, experience, discrimination, sophistication, and above all, curiosity is far wider than might be expected.

It may or may not be characteristic of all male cooks, but these men have done a good deal of talking in the course of getting their recipes down on paper. The anecdotes often set the stage for a recipe, and may even help you to pick the right occasion for preparing and serving it.

FEATS WITH MEATS

Men that cook are most likely to cook meats, for most males subscribe heartily to the dictum that a meal should be planned around a meat dish.

Men cook meats with good appetite. Sometimes there can be a distinction between lady-like servings and man-size servings. As one male sums up: "Makes six servings if dining, or four servings if really hungry."

In their daily work, men frequently wrestle with problems, and this problem-oriented line of thinking is often carried into the kitchen. Taking this approach to meat cooking, for example, they inquire first, "What's the problem? Does it have to do with texture, flavor, appearance, size?" Once the problem is identified, they somehow find it easier to figure out how to barbecue, bake, roast, boil, marinate, or sauce.

Since beef steak is an extremely popular meat (most men cooks have no problem with it; a man usually develops his own relatively simple formula for handling it and then stays with the formula), this chapter contains only a few steak recipes. The well-known cuts of beef, lamb, and pork are well represented. You may be intrigued by the recipes for such items as venison pot roast, lamb's tongues, sweetbreads, kidneys, rabbit, and baby goat.

🎞 American Special-Western Style 🎞

There is a touch of madness about this "American Special–Western Style," as Michael Minshull's wife insists, but another crazy thing about it is that the steak tastes surprisingly good after marinating in the far-out brew. You might just try it.

½ cup Kahlúa liqueur
3 teaspoons lemon juice
1 teaspoon salt
½ teaspoon ground pepper
2-pound piece sirloin steak, cut 1½ inches thick

Mix together the liqueur, lemon juice, salt, and pepper. Pour it over the steak, in a shallow pan, and marinate for 2 hours, turning occasionally. Grill over medium-hot coals about 8 inches above heat; about 8 minutes on a side for rare meat, or longer for medium or well done. Makes 4 servings.

🎞 Sirloin Steak Chow Vegetables 🎞

From B. L. Wong, speaking of Sirloin Steak Chow Vegetables: "Not deviating from the ancient Chinese philosophy that we live to eat and not eat to live, may I humbly submit the following kitchen-tested formula for your approval?"

Ginger is a strong and important flavor here, and both meat and peas should be done quickly over high heat so that they retain fresh flavor.

2 pounds sirloin steak, 1 inch thick
½ teaspoon salt
½ teaspoon monosodium glutamate
1 teaspoon sugar
1-inch piece fresh ginger, finely chopped or
mashed (about 1 tablespoon)
¼ cup soy sauce
¼ cup port wine
8 tablespoons salad oil
1 pound fresh mushrooms, sliced
1 package (7 oz.) frozen Chinese pea pods (with or
without water chestnuts), partly defrosted
1 pound fresh peas, shelled and rinsed (1 cup shelled peas)
2 small cans (5 oz. each) bamboo shoots,
drained and thinly sliced across grain
1 tablespoon cornstarch
⅓ cup water

Cut the meat into squares about 1 by 1 by ¼ inch. Combine the salt, monosodium glutamate, sugar, ginger, soy sauce, and port wine; set aside. Heat 4 tablespoons of the oil in a large frying pan or *wok* over high heat until it just begins to smoke. Add the beef and cook, stirring constantly, for 1 minute. Pour in the soy-wine mixture and bring just to boiling. Pour immediately into another container (to dissipate heat and prevent beef from cooking more).

Without washing the first pan, heat remaining 4 tablespoons oil. Add mushrooms and stir-fry for about 3 minutes. Strain into the pan the juices from the beef; then add the Chinese peas, shelled peas, and bamboo shoots. Cover the pan and cook about 3 minutes, until peas are tender. Blend the cornstarch with the water until smooth. Remove cover, and gradually stir cornstarch mixture into liquid in the pan. Cook, stirring, until thickened. Add the cooked beef and stir over heat just until beef is reheated. Serve immediately. Makes 8 servings.

⫷ **Steak Siciliano Broil** ⫸

The program for a meat sauce is simple: Heighten but don't overshadow the flavor of the meat. For any steak of your choice, here is an excellent combination from Hans Kaehler—"herby, winy, and woodsy," as one happy partaker put it.

1 cup Burgundy
1 small clove garlic, crushed
¼ teaspoon oregano
1 small onion, minced
1 teaspoon salt
¼ teaspoon pepper
1 tablespoon Worcestershire
2 tablespoons prepared horseradish
2 tablespoons minced parsley
2 tablespoons prepared mustard
1 tablespoon sugar
2 tablespoons butter
2½ pounds top sirloin steak, 1½ inches thick

Combine Burgundy, garlic, oregano, onion, salt, pepper, Worcestershire, horseradish, parsley, mustard, sugar, and butter. Heat until the butter is melted; let cool to room temperature. Pour sauce over steak (which should also be at room temperature) and marinate about 3 hours, turning occasionally. Remove meat. Broil, basting with marinade, about 7 minutes each side for medium rare. Makes about 6 servings.

⫷ **Sweet and Sour Short Ribs** ⫸

From Eugene R. Horner comes a meat dish that can be prepared in a Dutch oven and on the barbecue grill—or just in the Dutch oven alone. Some may prefer to increase the portion of vinegar so that the sweet and sour effect will be more noticeable.

3 pounds beef short ribs, cut into finger lengths
Salt and pepper
Flour
Shortening
1 cup sliced onions
1 clove garlic, minced
1¼ cups hot water
1 bay leaf
¼ cup vinegar
3 tablespoons brown sugar
⅓ cup catsup
½ teaspoon salt

When the short ribs are cut into finger lengths, they will shrink and drop away from the bone during cooking, leaving the right-sized serving pieces.

Sprinkle meat with salt and pepper, dredge with flour, and brown well on all sides in a small amount of shortening. Remove to Dutch oven. Cook onions and garlic in about 2 tablespoons shortening until soft; add to the ribs. Combine remaining ingredients and pour over ribs. Cover and simmer over low heat until about two-thirds done, about 1 hour. Drain well and place over coals, turning and browning until done. (Or if barbecuing is not convenient at the time, complete the cooking in the Dutch oven.) Makes about 4 to 6 servings.

✺ Lazy Man's Roast ✺

According to Curtis Ward, far too many recipes finish with the command, "Serve at once! Since my style of cooking does not readily lend itself to such precision timing, the following recipe has evolved. It allows the cooking to be done while I'm out digging weeds, and if I forget the time for an extra hour, no catastrophe results. Of course, the big dividend of such a recipe is leftovers—fine juicy sandwiches and snacks for the whole week."

3 to 4 pounds rump roast
1 cup claret or Burgundy
1½ teaspoons salt
10 whole black peppers
1½ tablespoons brown sugar (optional)
3 bay leaves
4 fresh sage leaves, crumbled, or about
½ teaspoon dried sage

Trim most of the fat from the meat and put it in a close-fitting kettle which has a tight-fitting lid. Then add the wine, salt, pepper, sugar, and herbs. Do *not* brown the meat. Cover and cook the meat 4 hours at a very gentle simmer. (With the relatively little liquid, it is important that the pan lid fit tightly so the pan won't become dry.)

Remove pan from heat and let meat set in the liquid at least an hour before serving (you can reheat if you want). Makes 6 to 8 servings.

✺ Korean Broil ✺

"In Tokyo there is a very popular restaurant that specializes in Korean food," says Dr. M. J. Rosten. "They give you a platter of small pieces of raw beef, a pair of chopsticks, and a lit hibachi. Everyone broils his own at each table. The meat is unusually delicious and after experimenting, I found the way to prepare it. The sesame oil may be obtained at any Oriental grocery."

Anyone who knows beef teriyaki will spot this as a near-cousin, stronger on garlic, with sesame instead of ginger. It would be great for hot hors d'oeuvres at a cocktail party on the patio, yet it's simple enough to prepare for a family dinner. You can marinate the beef much longer than we have indicated, but after about 30 minutes the marinade begins to obliterate the taste of meat.

1 pound top sirloin
¼ cup soy sauce
2 tablespoons sesame oil
¼ teaspoon garlic powder

Cut the meat into thin (about ⅛ inch) strips across the grain. Mix the remaining ingredients together; place meat in this marinade and leave for about 30 minutes at room temperature. Broil meat over hot coals or in an oven broiler, but do not overcook (1 minute or less on each side). Eat immediately. Makes 2 or 3 servings as an entrée, 6 or more as hors d'oeuvres.

⚹ Tortilla Flats ⚹

It's hard to avoid a little prejudice in favor of a recipe named Tortilla Flats. Fortunately, the taste of Andrew Matto's dish is also rewarding.

The name undoubtedly derives in part from the way some city buildings have rental "flats" one on top of another.

1½ pounds lean beef stew meat,
cut in about ½-inch cubes
1 tablespoon shortening or salad oil
1½ cups water
1 teaspoon salt
Pepper to taste
1 clove garlic, minced or crushed
1 tablespoon brown bottled gravy sauce
1 teaspoon oregano
1 tablespoon chile powder
1 can (4 oz.) peeled California green chiles,
seeded and chopped
1 can (1 lb.) solid pack tomatoes
8 (part of a package) flour tortillas
Shortening for frying
Sour cream (optional)

Place meat in a frying pan and brown in the 1 tablespoon shortening. Then add water, salt, pepper, garlic, gravy sauce, oregano, and chile powder. Cover and simmer slowly about 45 minutes, or until meat is tender. Add chiles and tomatoes and let cook down 15 minutes or so, or until mixture is getting a bit thick.

Meanwhile, quickly fry tortillas in about ½ inch of hot shortening until golden brown; put in a very slow oven (250°) to stay warm.

When ready to serve, put a tortilla on each plate, spoon over some of the meat mixture, put another tortilla on top, and spoon over meat mixture. Pass sour cream. Makes 4 hearty servings.

⚹ Call it Kid ⚹

In Saltillo, Mexico, when you ask about good local food, you always hear about *cabrito*. The favorite is Cabrito al Pastor (baby goat cooked sheepherder style—over the coals), and it is served in Saltillo all year.

In this country, people of Italian as well as Mexican descent traditionally serve baby goat, or kid, at Easter. The Italians call it *capretto*, and the Mexicans call it either *cabrito* or *chivito*.

Meanwhile, let's sample one version scouted out by F. P. Cronemiller: "It is a mild flavored meat in spite of the reputation of its pappy. It could be described as something between lamb and veal. It is tender and moist, and if you do not tell your guests it is goat, they will praise it."

Hindquarter of capretto (about 4 lbs.)
½ cup olive oil, or other salad oil
½ cup white wine
1 medium-sized onion, finely chopped
3 cloves garlic, finely chopped
⅓ cup finely chopped parsley
2 teaspoons finely chopped fresh or dried rosemary
1 small can (8 oz.) tomato sauce
2 teaspoons salt
½ teaspoon pepper
1 can (8 oz.) pitted ripe olives

Have the meatman cut capretto into small serving-sized pieces. Brown in oil. Add wine; simmer until wine has almost disappeared (about 10 minutes). Add onion, garlic, parsley, and rosemary to capretto along with tomato sauce, salt, and pepper. Simmer until capretto is almost tender or about 1 hour. Add olives and cook about 10 minutes more. Make gravy or a thickened sauce from the drippings, if you wish. Makes about 6 servings. Serve with potatoes, a green vegetable, and a green salad.

⚜ Ground Beef Oriental ⚜

East and West effect a meeting in Wallace S. Wharton's recipe for ground beef patties. These have a Japanese teriyaki taste and a Scandinavian meat ball texture—a fine combination indeed. Don't overcook; the rarer they are, the juicier they remain.

4 dried mushroom caps
Water
1 pound ground round steak
2 tablespoons soy sauce
1½ teaspoons ground ginger
1 light sprinkle cayenne pepper
1 sprinkle monosodium glutamate
2 tablespoons olive oil

Soak dried mushroom caps in water for 30 minutes to 1 hour. Place ground round in a bowl, make a crater in the middle, pour in the soy sauce, and sprinkle with ginger, cayenne pepper, and monosodium glutamate. Drain mushrooms, cut into pieces about ¼ inch square, and place in crater.

Mix the meat with all the other ingredients by hand until all are well distributed. Divide into three patties, each about ½ inch thick. Pour olive oil into a frying pan, and place over medium heat; when hot, put patties in; cook until browned on both sides and done to taste. Makes 3 servings.

⚜ Oxtails Marsala ⚜

"This is finger-eating food," Clyde L. Blohm states clearly, "and a bit messy—but good! Have plenty of paper napkins available." Considering the fanciness of the result, the ingredients are surprisingly inexpensive and readily available.

3 pounds oxtails, disjointed
Water to cover
1 large onion, quartered
1 teaspoon celery salt
1 clove garlic
1 tablespoon salt
1 teaspoon oregano
About 6 whole black peppers
Monosodium glutamate
3 tablespoons salad oil
1 cup Marsala wine
4 oz. (half an 8-oz. can) tomato sauce
1 tablespoon meat seasoning sauce
1 teaspoon sugar

Simmer oxtails in water with onion, celery salt, garlic, salt, oregano, and whole black peppers for 1 hour, or until meat is tender. Drain. Sprinkle oxtails generously with monosodium glutamate. Sauté in oil until thoroughly browned—don't do it over too high heat and run the risk of overbrowning them; drain off drippings. Add ¾ cup Marsala wine, cover, and simmer for 30 minutes, adding water, if needed, just to keep some liquid in the pan. Add tomato sauce, meat seasoning sauce, sugar, and other ¼ cup Marsala. Keep over low heat for another 10 minutes.

Remove sauce-covered oxtails and place on a platter to serve. Serve remaining sauce as an extra. Makes 4 to 6 servings, depending upon appetite.

❧ Pit-Cooked Pig ❧

There's a sorry dearth of ceremony in our lives. We need more excuses to shuck off the weary round. We don't lack occasions for celebration, we just need a richer variety of ways to celebrate them. So welcome to John M. Peat for picking an uncommon way—pit-cooked pig.

A word about the preparations. Pit cooking takes wood and wood and wood. If you buy your wood by the cord, better cook by electricity. On the other hand, you may indulge freely in this pyromania if you literally have wood to burn, or if you would like to precede this occasion with another: Once or twice a year, you could have a lot of fun organizing a firewood hunt with a gang bent on rounding up all unclaimed wood on the beach or in the nearby mountains or foothills.

With plenty of wood assured, take care to burn long enough to produce plenty of glowing coals. And overdo the cooking a little bit, if in doubt. The first time you try pit cooking you have to count as practice. Thereafter, you will grow wiser with every successive try.

Says John Peat, "Three 10 to 15-pound legs of fresh pork are normally needed to feed 40 or 50 people." All his recipe quantities read accordingly, and he recommends digging a pit 2 by 4 feet wide and 2 feet deep. For this recipe, however, you can use one leg of pork and cook in a pit slightly smaller than prescribed.

1 leg (10 to 15 lbs.) fresh pork

MARINADE

½ gallon dry sherry
⅓ cup soy sauce
1 can (6 oz.) frozen lime juice or frozen limeade
1 cup frozen or canned papaya, or about
half of a fresh papaya, mashed
1 or 2 small fingers of ginger root, grated or crushed
1 large clove garlic, peeled and crushed
3 tablespoons seasoning salt

Have the meatman bone and trim off all excess fat, then roll the meat. Mix together all marinade ingredients. Marinate meat overnight.

Start your fire in a rock-lined pit about 8 A.M., and by noon the pit should be full of glowing embers. Remove pork leg from marinade, wrap in ti leaves (available from florists), then in clean sheeting, then in burlap. Tie with wire, which serves as a handle. Saturate the burlap and sheeting with the remaining marinade, then bury the meat in coals. Cover the coals with sand and dirt until you no longer see any smoke.

Take the afternoon for swimming and resting for a big evening. About 8 P.M., remove meat and serve. Makes 16 to 24 servings, depending on appetites.

❧ Burgundy Beef ❧

The basic formula of Boeuf Bourguignon, or Burgundy beef, is of the utmost simplicity: Brown some cubes of beef, then simmer in Burgundy. You can add a great variety of other ingredients, and the simmering can take place either on top of the stove or inside the oven.

This version from B. J. Lyons isn't quite like most of the others. For one thing, he uses a little sherry in the early stages as well as a larger amount of Burgundy later. But what counts most is the end result, which many would rate at the top of its class.

2 pounds chuck, cut into 1-inch cubes
2 tablespoons butter or margarine
¼ cup sherry
½ pound mushrooms, quartered
6 tablespoons flour
2 teaspoons catsup
2 teaspoons bottled brown gravy sauce
2 cups water or stock
2 cups Burgundy
1 bay leaf
1 teaspoon fines herbs
Salt and pepper to taste
1 can (1 lb.) small whole onions, drained

Brown the beef in butter or margarine. Pour sherry over the beef, then remove it from pan with slotted spoon. Add mushrooms to pan; cook for 1 minute. Stir in flour, catsup, gravy sauce, and water. Cook, stirring, until mixture begins to boil. Return meat to pan and add 1 cup of Burgundy and remaining seasonings.

Place onions on top of meat, so they will hold their shape. Cover pan and simmer 2 to 2½ hours, until meat is tender, adding remaining cup of Burgundy as needed. Makes 4 to 6 servings, depending upon appetites. A batch of mashed potatoes or crusty French bread to absorb the extra gravy is a must.

❧ Steak Beer-Gers ❧

Beer in the burgers? Why not? Wine has been used in them for years. As Donald E. Torrence uses it here, the beer is not noticeable in the final taste (unless you concentrate on it intently). But it does contribute an interesting overtone.

If you barbecue these "beer-gers" over charcoal, arrange the coals in an outer circle and place the meat inside so the bacon drippings won't cause heavy smoke. It is also a good idea to use quite thinly sliced bacon and cook only until the bacon is done—to avoid overcooking the beef inside.

2 pounds freshly ground sirloin or chuck steak
Salt and pepper to taste
½ can (6 oz.) beer, at room temperature
3 tablespoons butter or margarine
6 slices bacon

Gently mix meat, salt, pepper, and beer, and shape into 6 large patties. Spread both sides of each one with butter; then wrap each with bacon and secure with toothpicks. Broil over charcoal or under oven broiler. Makes 6 servings.

ᨏ Lapin en Gibelotte ᨏ

Halsey Stevens, teacher at the University of Southern California School of Music, and composer of note, also creates harmony in the kitchen. Says he: "There must be as many versions of *Lapin en Gibelotte* in France as there are *gulyás* in Hungary. Some call for tomato paste; others require potatoes and onions. The essential ingredients, however, are rabbit and wine. The recipe that follows is not an adaptation of an existing recipe, but a personal creation from a given set of premises."

A personal creation is the kind we honor most in this company, of course. And in this case, the crowning achievement is certainly the sauce. Chicken—or really almost any other fowl, meat, or fish—would taste good in it.

1 rabbit (3 to 4 lbs.)
¼ cup (½ cube) butter
¼ cup salad oil
1 clove garlic
12 small white onions
12 fresh mushrooms
1 stalk celery, chopped
1 sprig parsley, chopped
1 sprig fresh basil, or ½ teaspoon dry basil
1 bay leaf
1 teaspoon salt
¼ teaspoon pepper
2 tablespoons flour
1 cup dry white wine
1 cup water
Steamed rice

Cut rabbit into serving pieces. Heat butter, oil, and garlic; brown rabbit on all sides and then remove to casserole. In the same fat, brown whole onions and mushrooms (both caps and stems). Add the onions, celery, parsley, basil, bay, salt, and pepper to the casserole. Discard garlic; set mushrooms aside.

Stir flour into the fat to make a *roux*; gradually add wine and water, stirring to prevent lumps. Cook until slightly thickened, pour over rabbit and onions, cover, and bake 30 minutes in moderate oven (350°). Remove, add mushrooms, cover again, and return to oven for 20 to 30 minutes longer, or until rabbit and onions are tender.

Serve with steamed rice and the sauce from the casserole. A green salad is all the accompaniment needed. Makes 3 to 4 servings.

❧ The Flavor of Green Chiles ❧

Bill Parkins says of this recipe: "I think you will find I have obtained a desired degree of sophistication in the measurements, but do not get the idea that a ruler is my most important kitchen utensil. The dish has a distinct flavor of green chiles, quite different from the muddy flavor of red chiles which the word chile usually conjures up in our minds."

The flavors of several ingredients are assertive, but the over-all effect is pleasant.

2 dozen fresh mushrooms of 1-inch diameter
About ¼ cup (½ cube) butter
1 can (4 oz.) green chiles
8 green onions
1 flank steak (about 1½ pounds)
½ teaspoon thyme
½ teaspoon coarse-ground pepper
Garlic powder
Salt
½ pound packaged egg noodles
4 teaspoons flour
¾ cup dry vermouth
1 cup water

Cut mushrooms in ⅛-inch slices. Brown lightly in about 2 tablespoons of the butter and set aside. After removing seeds, cut chiles into ⅛-inch slices; add to mushrooms uncooked. Slice bulbs of onions into ⅛-inch slices and add to chiles and mushrooms.

Thinly slice flank steak across grain diagonally. Heat remaining butter in a large frying pan. Put in meat; season with thyme, pepper, garlic powder, and salt to taste; fry quickly just until browned, about 1 minute on each side. Remove from pan and keep warm. Put noodles in boiling salted water; cook until tender.

Blend flour with mixture of vermouth and water; pour into the frying pan and stir until smooth; add mushrooms, chiles, and onions, and cook, stirring until sauce is slightly thickened. Add steak, cover pan, and cook just until heated through, about 2 minutes. Pour mixture over drained noodles and serve with a tossed salad. Makes 6 servings.

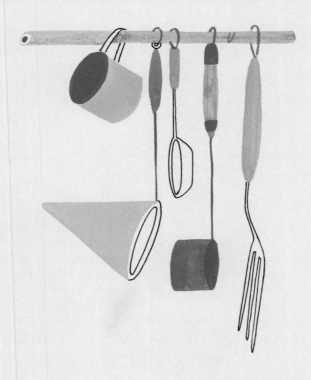

ꙮ Beef with Eye Appeal ꙮ

F. E. Blacklidge says: "A friend's recipe for Chinese Beef and Peppers called for lean beef sliced very thin and cut into strips about two inches long. I made it that way a few times and then decided to try it with ground beef. It hasn't the eye appeal of sliced beef but tastes every bit as good." You might wish to add a little bright color with sliced red pepper. If you cook with your eyes (for the eye), go ahead. Any dish tastes better if it looks good.

1½ pounds ground beef
1 clove garlic, mashed
2 tablespoons salad oil
1 teaspoon salt
½ teaspoon pepper
½ teaspoon grated fresh or crystallized ginger
1¾ cups water
2 beef bouillon cubes
1 bunch green onions, with tops,
cut into ¼-inch lengths
4 green peppers, cut into ½-inch squares
4 large stalks celery, cut diagonally
into ¼-inch strips
¼ cup water
2 tablespoons cornstarch
1 tablespoon soy sauce
Steamed rice

Brown beef and garlic lightly in oil in a deep kettle; then pour off fat. Break meat into bite-sized pieces and season with salt, pepper, and ginger. Add water and bouillon cubes and simmer 15 minutes. Add all three vegetables and cook over medium heat, stirring continuously, 4 to 6 minutes or until thoroughly heated. Combine ¼ cup water, cornstarch, and soy sauce into a smooth paste; add to mixture. Cover and cook, stirring frequently, until celery is tender.

Serve very hot over steamed rice. Put soy sauce on the table and let each diner add to suit his taste. Makes 6 servings.

ꙮ Authoritative Corned Beef ꙮ

In order to enjoy corned beef, you don't need to put it through the four-hour preparation that Eugene Horner suggests for it. But if you do go along with him, you won't regret it. The corned beef takes on a beautiful red color and acquires delectably authoritative flavor.

About 4 pounds corned beef eye of the
round, or your favorite cut
1 clove garlic
2 tablespoons mixed pickling spices
¼ cup soy sauce
¼ cup salad oil
2 teaspoons prepared mustard

Place corned beef in Dutch oven, add garlic and pickling spices, and simmer in water to cover for 1½ to 2 hours. Remove, drain, put on spit, and cook over coals for 2 hours or more, basting frequently with mixture of soy sauce, oil, and mustard. Makes 10 ample and hearty servings.

MEAT—THE MAIN THEME

"This dish of meat is too good for any but anglers, or very honest men," Izaak Walton said, probably on a day the fish weren't biting. Some men who cook are anglers and others are honest men, but all are worthy tasters of a dish of meat.

In food knowledge and sophistication, men who really like to cook have little in common with Meat-and-Potatoes Charlie, who's kind of passé, anyhow. Yet they fully understand why a meal is planned around the meat dish. It's the main theme; all else is counterpoint.

One kind of meat cookery calls for short cooking time and a minimum of handling to keep natural flavor and juices pretty much intact. Then there's another kind that sets no such limits; any amount of handling, cooking, or saucing is permissible if the results are good. In general, the first approach tends to be used with the choicer cuts of meat, and the second is used for the bargain cuts. This, however, isn't an invariable rule, for some classic dishes give the choicest cuts some quite elaborate preparation.

Turkish Beef Exotique

Nasturtiums on the menu are nothing new; in days gone by, many a housewife put up the seeds in pickle to use in place of capers. The contemporary nasturtium is bigger and handsomer than the simple little flower of long ago, but the pungent odor is there still, and in the recipe below, you don't have to wait for seeds to form.

John Bradbury picks the youngest leaves and freshly opened flowers as a garnish for a colorful beef and rice dish with overtones of the Middle East. You should allow two or three leaves and a flower for each person; or put just enough greenery on the beef to decorate it, and add nasturtium leaves and flowers to a green salad to go with it.

If you're in the habit of spraying your plants, be sure to use a spray designated for vegetable crops, and don't use it just before picking.

2 tablespoons butter or margarine
1 small onion, minced
1 clove garlic, minced or mashed
½ pound lean ground beef
1 beef bouillon cube dissolved in ¼ cup hot water
¼ teaspoon paprika
½ can (6-oz. size) tomato paste
½ teaspoon allspice
½ teaspoon salt
¼ teaspoon black pepper
3 tablespoons sherry or 1½ tablespoons wine vinegar
Turmeric rice (recipe follows)
Nasturtium leaves and flowers

Melt butter or margarine in a frying pan and sauté onion and garlic until golden. Add meat and stir until well separated and lightly browned. Mix paprika, tomato paste, allspice, salt, and pepper with bouillon mixture and add, stirring constantly. Add sherry or vinegar, and stir until liquid is nearly gone. Serve in a ring of turmeric rice, garnished with nasturtium leaves and flowers.

Turmeric Rice

Prepare ½ cup long grained white rice as directed on the package for steaming, adding ¼ teaspoon salt, ½ teaspoon salad oil, and ⅓ teaspoon turmeric. When done, turn into lightly greased ring mold, cool slightly, turn out, and fill with beef.

Makes 2 servings.

⚛ Hamburgers a la Phoops ⚛

Hamburger à la Phoops is what Wayne Phelps calls this recipe. The detail that stands out is a small amount of Roquefort crumbled into the meat before cooking. The creator was reticent about the exact amount, but wifely arguments finally prevailed.

¼ pound Roquefort or blue cheese
3 pounds ground chuck or lean ground beef
½ cup minced chives or green onions
including tops
¼ teaspoon liquid hot-pepper seasoning
1 teaspoon Worcestershire
1 teaspoon coarse-ground pepper
1½ teaspoons salt
1 teaspoon dry mustard
12 French rolls or hamburger buns

Crumble cheese into meat. Add chives, liquid hot-pepper seasoning, Worcestershire, pepper, salt, mustard, and mix together lightly. Let stand 2 hours to give flavors time to blend; then lightly press the meat into about 12 patties; broil or barbecue until browned on both sides and done the way you like them. Serve on toasted and buttered French rolls or buns. Makes 12 hamburgers.

⚛ Freshly Minted Meatballs ⚛

The man who plucked the mint out of the julep glass is William Tapia. He has this to say about his discovery: "Freshly picked mint is an absolute requirement. If you don't have a mint bed already in your herb garden, run out to the nursery and buy a plant. It's well worth the extra effort."

These meatballs are two-thirds beef and one-third lamb. The quantity of mint given here imparts a delicate, just discernible flavor.

1 pound lean ground beef
½ pound lean ground lamb
1½ tablespoons finely chopped fresh mint
½ cup fresh bread crumbs
2 eggs
1 medium-sized onion, finely chopped
1¼ teaspoons salt
⅛ teaspoon pepper
Flour
6 tablespoons salad oil
1 can (1 lb.) tomatoes
½ teaspoon sweet basil

Mix the ground beef and lamb, or have the meatman grind both kinds of meat together. Wash and finely chop mint leaves and stems, and add 1 tablespoon to the meat mixture, together with the bread crumbs, eggs, onion, salt, and pepper. Blend and shape into balls about 1½ inches in diameter. Roll the balls in flour. Heat the oil and then brown the meatballs. When meatballs are well browned, pour off excess fat and add tomatoes, sweet basil, remaining ½ tablespoon mint, and salt and pepper to taste, if needed. Cover and cook 15 minutes, or until done. Makes about 4 to 6 servings.

⚜ Sophisticated Lamb-Burger ⚜

To the broiling of hamburger, and variations thereof, there is no end. But here is a variation that may surprise you.

"We think of hamburger as something people balance their budgets by using," says Eugene R. Horner. "Therefore we have never served hamburgers to guests. We just don't think it's fair to them. We serve this delicious recipe instead."

1½ pounds of ground lamb
½ teaspoon garlic salt
½ cup chopped green onions and some of the tops
4 tablespoons cocktail sherry
1 teaspoon salt
½ teaspoon oregano

Mix lamb thoroughly with garlic salt, onion, sherry, salt, and oregano. Gently shape into patties and broil about 5 minutes on each side. Keep on rare side for best flavor. Serve with mint jelly in place of the usual barbecue sauce, catsup and pickles, or other condiments. Makes 4 servings.

⚜ Pyrenean Leg of Lamb ⚜

"This dish was learned from my mother-in-law many years ago," says Franz R. Sachse, "and is a favorite in the French Pyrenees. I've never seen or heard of it elsewhere, and it has never failed to produce amazed compliments."

2 cups small white navy beans
Cold water
2 large onions
2 bay leaves
6 to 8 whole black peppers
2 teaspoons salt
¼ teaspoon rosemary
¼ teaspoon thyme
¼ teaspoon oregano
5-pound leg of lamb
2 cloves garlic

Soak beans overnight in cold water to cover. The next day add water to barely cover the beans; add onions, quartered, and bay leaves, crumbled, and all other ingredients except lamb and garlic. Cover and cook slowly over low heat or in the oven (a 300° oven is ideal) for about 3 hours. They must never get mushy. Stir occasionally, and add water if necessary to prevent burning, but when finished, the beans should have absorbed almost all of the water.

Prepare the leg of lamb by crushing the garlic in a press and thoroughly rubbing the outside. Salt and pepper to taste and roast as you prefer. (For slightly rare, about 32 minutes per pound.)

When the roast is done, remove to a platter and keep warm. Dump the beans, water, onions, and everything into the lamb juices in the roasting pan; stir to mix thoroughly, and cook about 30 minutes.

There it is. With a tossed salad and red wine, it will make any guest take notice. Makes 6 to 8 servings. Incidentally, if there is anything left, cut the lamb from the bone in chunks, add to the beans, and heat in a casserole for a fine one-dish meal.

Veal Scallopini A.R.P.A.

If the most sophisticated person of your acquaintance should come to dinner, your reputation for savoir faire is secure if you serve Veal Scallopini. And you will look a long time before you find a recipe for this dish that is both so easy and excellent as the one proposed by H. J. Longfelder. He confesses he had powerful stimulus for this burst of creativity:

"While on a year's assignment working for the Advanced Research Projects Agency (A.R.P.A.) in Washington, D. C., I decided one night to create a new Veal Scallopini recipe as an antidote to working in the Pentagon."

2 pounds thinly sliced veal
Flour
2 tablespoons butter
¼ cup olive oil
½ cup chopped green onions
1 teaspoon extract of beef
1 cup chicken stock
¼ teaspoon monosodium glutamate
Pepper to taste
¼ teaspoon oregano
¼ teaspoon rosemary
2 tablespoons finely chopped parsley
½ pound fresh mushrooms, sliced and
previously browned in butter
¼ to ½ cup Marsala wine

Pound veal thoroughly on both sides, dredge in flour, and brown in the butter and olive oil. Remove veal from pan, place in an ovenproof dish, and set in warm oven (250°).

Meanwhile add to drippings in pan all remaining ingredients except mushrooms and wine. Simmer about 10 minutes; then add veal, mushrooms, and ¼ cup of the Marsala wine. Simmer for approximately 5 minutes longer, adding a little more Marsala wine for flavor about 2 minutes before serving. Serve on top of wild rice if feeling quite elegant; otherwise, on plain rice. Makes 4 servings.

⚒ Barbecued Leg of Lamb ⚒

On his backyard barbecue, Paul C. Nelson likes to roast a boned leg of lamb with a few bits of garlic stuffed inside.

Lamb, even the succulent spring variety, is often a subject of controversy. There are those who hold for pinkness and those who shudder at anything less than well done. If you win the battle for the color you prefer, the best way to be assured of getting it is to use a meat thermometer. Temperatures for medium rare, medium well, and well done are given below.

Chef Nelson's lamb takes 24 hours to prepare. You begin with a boned leg of lamb and a marinade, and end with a very special feed.

1 leg of lamb (about 5 lbs.), boned
1 onion
2 cloves garlic
2 teaspoons salt
¾ teaspoon pepper
¼ teaspoon cayenne
2 teaspoons oregano
½ cup red wine or red wine vinegar
½ cup olive oil or salad oil

Ask your meatman to bone the leg of lamb, but do not roll and tie. One day ahead of cooking, prepare the marinade in a large, deep dish. Slice the onion very thinly and line the bottom of dish. Spread the lamb out flat with the skin side down and generously scatter slivers of garlic over the cut side, then season with half the salt, pepper, cayenne, and oregano. Turn the lamb into the dish, cut side down, and put remaining garlic, salt, pepper, cayenne, and oregano on the skin side.

Pour the wine and oil over the meat, and marinate overnight, basting occasionally.

Before cooking, remove the lamb from the marinade, line the cut side with a few garlic pieces, roll, and tie. Spit the meat; insert meat thermometer into the center (be sure it is not touching the spit), and roast over medium coals to 145°-150° for medium rare, 160°-165° for medium well, and 175°-180° for well done. Baste occasionally with the marinade.

⚞ Butterflied Leg of Lamb ⚟

The three most important ingredients in this recipe are the curry powder, garlic, and oregano; they give sterling character to the marinade. Purely incidental are the needs for Chablis wine to provide the liquid, and a leg of lamb for which Lloyd Bryan thought up the whole beautiful concoction.

Your meatman will bone and butterfly the leg of lamb if you ask him. But if you forget to ask, or if you enjoy playing amateur butcher, the job isn't difficult to do yourself. With a boning knife or any sharp and preferably narrow-bladed knife, cut as close to the bone as possible. After the bone is removed, make as few cuts as necessary to make the meat spread out rather flat.

    1 large leg of lamb, about 6½ to 7 pounds
        with bone in
    2 teaspoons salt
    ½ teaspoon pepper
    1½ tablespoons curry powder
    1½ tablespoons whole oregano
    1 tablespoon minced garlic
    1 bottle (4/5 quart) Chablis wine

Bone and butterfly the leg of lamb, or have your meatman do it. Combine salt, pepper, curry, oregano, and garlic. Rub the meat all over with the seasonings, to get maximum coverage and penetration. Put the meat in a bowl of adequate size but no larger than necessary; cover it with Chablis and marinate at least 5 or 6 hours or overnight.

Drain and place on barbecue grill over hot fire to sear both sides. Then move farther away from fire and slow-cook for 45 minutes to 1 hour or until a meat thermometer registers 140° in the thickest part for medium rare. (Cook longer for medium.) Turn each time the meat gets shiny on top. Makes 8 or more servings; is also wonderful cold.

⚞ Mary's Lamb ⚟

One might conjecture on why A. L. Marshall calls this Mary's Lamb, but suffice it to say neck of lamb—with well-chosen accompaniments—makes good eating.

    4 thick lamb neck slices
    Flour seasoned with salt and freshly ground pepper
    3 tablespoons olive oil
    1 clove garlic, chopped
    2 tablespoons flour
    ½ cup broth or bouillon (or water)
    1 cup red wine
    1 medium-sized onion, peeled, with a
        bay leaf pinned to it with 2 cloves
    ½ teaspoon sweet marjoram

Trim skin and fat from edges of the lamb neck slices, wipe them with a dampened paper towel, and dust with the seasoned flour. Heat olive oil and garlic in a heavy frying pan; brown lamb nicely on both sides and edges. Remove to casserole.

To the pan in which you browned the lamb, add the 2 tablespoons flour; cook, stirring, until bubbly. Stir in broth, wine, onion with bay leaf and cloves, and marjoram. Cook, stirring, until smooth. Continue cooking for a minute or two, then pour over the lamb in the casserole. Cover and bake in a slow oven (300°) about 2 hours, or until done. Makes 4 servings.

⚜ **Kebabs with Compliments** ⚜

Philip Von Phul is an ardent practitioner of the art of barbecuing; so ardent that he remodeled his garden to broaden his theater of operations. He has spread himself over a broad, two-level patio. He uses the upper level for cooking, while his guests sit around the lower-level firepit and watch hungrily.

This shish-kebab recipe combines elements of showmanship, simplicity, and fine flavor. Anyone can do it—but be prepared for compliments.

1 leg of lamb (about 5 lbs.) boned and
cut in 1½-inch chunks
1 cup olive oil
1½ cups red wine
2 tablespoons wine vinegar
1 teaspoon salt
2 cloves garlic, crushed, or
2 teaspoons garlic powder
¼ cup chopped parsley
½ teaspoon oregano
1 teaspoon thyme
2 cans (1 lb. each) small whole onions, drained
1 can (8 oz.) whole mushrooms, drained

Have your meatman bone, skin, and cut up the leg of lamb. The day before barbecuing, mix oil, wine, vinegar, salt, garlic, parsley, oregano, and thyme in a deep bowl. Add lamb and leave overnight.

Arrange meat on skewers, alternating with onions, and mushrooms, and putting meat pieces first and last on the skewers. Allow 4 or 5 chunks of meat per skewer. Broil 12 to 15 minutes over hot coals, turning frequently, and basting with the marinade. Makes 8 to 10 servings.

⚜ **Pork Chop Riesling** ⚜

"Cooking is an avocation of mine," says lawyer Harlan P. Huebner. His bid is a treatment of pork chops that has inspired comments like "inspired combination" and "exceptionally tasty." Let the ingredients speak for themselves.

10 to 12 pork chops
1 can (10½ oz.) condensed celery soup
(do not add water)
1 small can (3 or 4 oz.) mushrooms
¾ cup Riesling wine
Salt
Pepper
Garlic salt
About 1 tablespoon prepared blend of Italian herbs

In a frying pan, brown pork chops on both sides, then arrange in a baking pan. In a separate bowl, mix celery soup and mushrooms (including their liquid) with the wine; blend in salt, pepper, and garlic salt to taste. Pour mixture over the pork chops. Sprinkle Italian herbs over chops. Bake in moderate oven (350°) for 1 hour, turning chops over and basting after first half hour. Remove chops to platter, pour remaining juice over them, and serve with a crisp, green salad. Makes 10 to 12 servings.

ꙮ Ham Banan ꙮ

"Ham used to be strong-flavored, smoke-house pork," muses H. R. Paradise. "But science has pushed on, and for all I know there are pigs in Louisiana smoking sugar-cane cheroots, sweet-curing themselves on the hoof.

"Anyway, ham has changed for the sweeter and tenderer, until it's more of a confection than a meat. They ought to sell it in candy stores. There used to be a coconut candy that mimicked ham slices, come to think of it.

"Far from fighting this drift, I am going along with it. I like sweet ham, and here is an ultimate just short of cloy."

3-pound center-cut ham slice
6 whole cloves
4 tablespoons brown sugar
2 tablespoons prepared mustard
Juice of 2 grapefruits
4 ripe bananas
Additional brown sugar

Festoon ham with cloves. Butter it with a mixture of sugar, mustard, and grapefruit juice. Bake in shallow pan for 50 minutes at 300°; baste frequently with the drippings. Remove, cover with banana slices, sprinkle with additional brown sugar, and bake another 10 to 15 minutes. Slice and serve. Makes 6 to 8 servings.

ꙮ Long-Soak Spareribs ꙮ

"The thing that determines the goodness of spareribs is the potency of the sauce, and you could smear it on your fingers and they'd taste as good," says one male cook.

He has a point, but it's oversimplified by far. What determines the goodness of spareribs is how successfully you minimize and counteract the fatness of the meat with sharp flavors, sweet flavors, and the application of heat.

Bud Getschman's spareribs get their rich fruity flavor, good color, and crustiness from a good, long sojourn in the marinade and a leisurely oven roasting.

4 to 5 pounds (about 2 sides) spareribs

MARINADE
¾ cup soy sauce
¾ cup orange marmalade
½ cup pineapple juice
2 teaspoons lemon juice
¼ teaspoon rosemary
2 large cloves garlic, finely chopped
1 teaspoon ginger
¼ teaspoon black pepper

Marinate the ribs in the marinade (simply mix all ingredients) for 10 to 12 hours. Arrange ribs on rack in roasting pan and roast for 1½ hours in a moderate oven (350°), basting frequently with marinade, until ribs are glazed golden brown and the meat is very tender. Cut ribs into finger-sized pieces and serve hot. Makes 6 to 10 servings.

Finger-Lickin' Spareribs

Perhaps you tire of eating elegantly so endlessly. In that case, the great American school of hearty cookery affords some famous antidotes, such as this one submitted by Quentin E. Smith.

"Up here in central Oregon's ponderosa pine country," says he, "we work up hearty appetites, so don't try this if you're not in the mood for some good serious eating. (A tripled recipe is great for a crowd on a nippy evening.) That sliced lemon is the special touch that cuts the heavy, greasy after-feel that many pork dishes have, so while these spareribs are as good warmed over as when piping hot, there seldom are any left to warm over."

The spareribs are remarkably un-fat, and have a rich flavor and an attractive reddish brown glaze.

6 pounds country-style spareribs
½ cup sherry
½ cup water

SAUCE

1 teaspoon salt
⅛ teaspoon pepper
¼ lemon, thinly sliced
½ cup finely chopped onion
1 teaspoon chile
1 teaspoon celery seed
¼ cup vinegar
¼ cup Worcestershire
1 cup catsup
½ cup brown sugar
2 cups water

In a large frying pan, brown spareribs (without flour). Then add sherry and ½ cup water and cook, covered, for 1 hour. In another pan, combine all sauce ingredients and cook for 1 hour.

Let spareribs cool in liquid long enough so you can skim off fat. Then remove spareribs and drain. Lay drained spareribs in large shallow casserole or roaster. Cover with the already-cooked sauce and bake 1 hour in a slow oven (300°). Bring to table in piping hot casserole, accompanied by rice or whipped potatoes, and a large mixed green salad. Makes 6 servings if dining; or makes 4 servings if really hungry.

✺ Saki Sauerkraut Spareribs ✺

Combining sauerkraut, spareribs, and saki (Japanese rice wine), this recipe takes the sharpness out of sauerkraut and the greasiness out of spareribs in a way that pleases most devotees of both.

Ed Colby says, "This is not a dish for those who want to keep thin." But it is not excessively loaded with calories (they come with that butter and French bread).

2 pounds pork spareribs
4 cups water
1 teaspoon salt
6 bay leaves
1 onion, chopped
3 tablespoons dehydrated vegetable flakes
2 cans (1 lb., 12 oz. each) sauerkraut, drained
2 cups saki
2 teaspoons monosodium glutamate
1 to 3 teaspoons caraway seed

Place spareribs in water, salt lightly, and add 3 of the bay leaves, the onion, and dehydrated vegetables. Bring to a boil, then turn down to simmer for about 4 hours or until meat is beginning to be tender but nowhere near the stage of falling off the bones.

About two hours before you plan on eating, remove pork from broth and skim fat off broth; reserve. In a large pan, combine sauerkraut, saki, monosodium glutamate, the other 3 bay leaves, the caraway, and 3 cups of the pork broth in which the spareribs were cooked. Lay spareribs on top, clamp a lid on the pan, and cook very slowly for two hours. Serve with lightly toasted French bread that has been lavishly spread with garlic butter. Makes 6 servings.

✺ Pickled Country-Style Ribs ✺

When you take pains to prepare a delectable sauce for spareribs, it's wise to have enough meat on those bones to make your efforts worthwhile. You should have very lean, meaty spareribs to match the sweet and spicy sauce that J. Richard Scheimer puts on them.

These aren't really pickled, as the name would indicate; they're just flavored with pickling spices.

1½ pounds lean country-style spareribs, cut into bite-sized pieces
1 cup water
2 tablespoons catsup
1 tablespoon corn syrup
1 teaspoon brown bottled gravy sauce
½ teaspoon salt
1 teaspoon pickling spices, wrapped in a cheesecloth bag

Spread ribs in a baking pan. Combine all other ingredients; pour over meat and marinate 1 to 2 hours. Roast in a moderate oven (350°) for 1 hour or until browned to your liking. Turn the ribs and baste with the sauce in the pan about every 15 minutes. Makes 2 servings.

✳ Push-Pan Liver ✳

If this book were to bestow anything like a "best-of-show" award, Bixelë Bialiej's recipe would be a prime contender.

The commendation is well expressed by one happy partaker: "Probably the best-prepared and tastiest liver I've ever eaten—and I am not ordinarily a liver enthusiast."

The liver is flavored delicately but distinctively. Yet the method is so simple and foolproof that you don't need to measure exact quantities.

Sliced calves liver or baby beef liver
Tarragon red wine vinegar
Salt and coarsely ground pepper
Olive oil
Butter

Have the sliced liver ready, and the tarragon red wine vinegar within quick reaching distance. While heating a heavy frying pan, copiously salt and pepper both sides of liver. Lubricate pan with a small amount of olive oil and an equal amount of butter. Sear liver quickly on one side, sprinkle with vinegar, and push slices around pan to acquire a dark glaze. Turn slices quickly, turn up heat, and repeat same treatment on other side. Use only enough vinegar so the residue makes a very small, pungent sauce to pour over liver on service plate.

Serve with a baked potato and a green salad.

✳ Kapika-Pau'a ✳

Now let us praise the man who knows how to get the grand effect with the slightest of efforts. Or, to put it another way, it is not mandatory that every recipe contain at least sixteen ingredients. Henry Vasconcellos did his culinary good turn with one special condiment borrowed from the Chinese—well worth having on your kitchen shelf for an occasional special effect.

Henry, who hails from Honolulu, often cooks up Kapika-Pau'a (translated Cabbage-Pork), for fishing companions. He uses ginger, soy, and sugar, too, but the really distinctive flavor is furnished by Chinese Five Spices (or Heong Lew Fun), which you can probably find only in a Chinese grocery store. Since different brands of soy sauce are apt to vary in saltiness, the original specifications have been cut back to a slightly more conservative figure. But be more generous if that suits your taste better.

Salad oil
2 pounds boneless fresh pork butt, cut into ¼-inch
slivers (or any thin-sliced lean pork)
1 teaspoon powdered ginger
½ cup soy sauce
2 teaspoons sugar
½ teaspoon Chinese Five Spices (Heong Lew Fun)
½ cup water
1 firm, medium-sized head of cabbage, shredded

Use enough oil to cover bottom of deep pan. Add pork; brown and cook it until partially done. Add ginger, soy sauce, sugar, Five Spices, and water. Simmer for 10 minutes. Add shredded cabbage, cover, and steam until cabbage is tender, about 10 minutes. Serve with rice. Makes 4 servings.

❧ Improved Venison Pot Roast ❧

John S. Morton, III does a little mumbling into his beard about the hunters who don't cool and age venison properly. "A week or two at near-freezing will produce much better meat if it can be arranged, so do the best you can."

However, he realizes that conditions aren't always optimum. "If it's too late or too much trouble, let's get on with a cooking method that will definitely improve whatever you have to work with. Quantities are based on a 2 or 3-pound chunk of hind quarter or shoulder, about 6 by 6 by 4 inches, something like a double handful of solid meat. If you do your own butchering and your estimating is as questionable as mine, these units may help. But have no fear, as the quantity of meat is not critical. I've used the recipe equally successfully with old bucks and small forked-horns."

You could also use beef in this dish, but the venison is responsible for its particularly rich flavor.

**About 3 pounds hind quarter or
shoulder of venison**
¼ cup (½ cube) butter or margarine
4 cubes beef bouillon
2 cups water
½ teaspoon salt
¼ teaspoon freshly ground pepper
2 tablespoons catsup
1 bay leaf
1 can (6 or 8 oz.) sliced mushrooms
¾ cup sherry (or red wine)
2 tablespoons flour

Brown the meat thoroughly on all sides in butter. While turning the meat for browning, dissolve bouillon in water and add salt, pepper, catsup, bay leaf, mushrooms, and ½ cup of the sherry; simmer while meat continues to brown. When meat is browned, pour over it ¼ cup sherry; remove meat and set aside.

Stir to blend the sherry with the browning ingredients left in the pan; add the flour and stir until bubbly. Gradually stir in the bouillon mixture.

Put meat back in pan, cover, and simmer for 1 hour. Remove and slice to serve with gravy from the pan. Makes 6 to 8 servings.

⚡ Kidneys Bavarian ⚡

Some dishes, however tasty and well turned, never appeal to a mass audience. Fortunately, individuals have infinite horizons of taste tolerance. However, even among the most adventurous eaters the word "kidney" is likely to cause a certain number to flee. Be assured that George A. Kern's recipe for the same is a very good one and let him carry it from there.

"This recipe is an old German recipe from Bavaria. I am sure you will agree that few recipes can compare with it in providing a tasty, vitamin-rich, well balanced, inexpensive dinner for six. Furthermore the entire dinner can be prepared in 30 minutes once you've done it a few times."

2 medium-sized beef kidneys (about 2 lbs.)
3 tablespoons bacon drippings, or
fat rendered from salt pork
1½ teaspoons salt
4 medium-sized onions, thinly sliced
½ cup white wine vinegar
½ cup hot water
2 tablespoons sugar
2 bay leaves
¼ teaspoon freshly ground pepper
3 tablespoons flour
1 tablespoon butter
Mashed potatoes or rice

Refrigerate kidneys until very cold to make slicing easier. Slice very thin, trimming away fat and connective tissue. Heat bacon drippings in a heavy frying pan, sprinkle kidneys with salt, and sauté until all red color disappears, about 5 minutes. Add onions, vinegar, hot water, sugar, bay leaves, and pepper, and bring quickly to a boil, stirring constantly.

Reduce heat, cover, and simmer very gently for 10 minutes, or until kidneys are tender. Blend flour with melted butter and add some of the liquid from the kidneys, blending until smooth. Return the flour mixture to frying pan and stir over low heat until sauce is thickened. Remove bay leaves and serve with mashed potatoes or rice. Makes about 6 to 8 servings.

❦ Forty Thieves Ham Steaks ❦

Why Kenneth Melrose developed a new barbecue recipe is a good subject:

"For the past 25 years or more, we have had a group of business and professional men who call themselves 'The 40 Thieves'. The principal object of this group is the enjoyment of each other's company at a barbecued dinner cooked in its entirety out of doors.

"The usual dinner consists of steaks or chicken, with a variation one meeting of butterfly legs of lamb, and another meeting a lobster barbecue. A few of us decided that the usual fare was becoming somewhat monotonous. After several tries I was able to put across my idea of barbecued ham steaks."

One of the "thieves" summed up "Ali Baba" Melrose's accomplishment justly in these words: "I'm not crazy about ham but this is delicious." It has good color, a beautiful glaze, and smoky-sweet flavor.

> 2 center-cut ham steaks, ¾ to 1 inch thick
> ½ cup currant jelly
> ½ cup red wine
> 1 tablespoon prepared mustard

Grill the ham over a rather hot fire, high enough above the coals so the steaks do not burn. This should take 30 to 45 minutes.

While the steaks cook, heat the jelly, wine, and mustard until the jelly is thoroughly melted. When the steaks are done, put in a pan and pour the jelly mixture over them. Cover and allow to simmer 30 minutes on a cool part of the grill. Cut each steak into two or three pieces and serve with some of the sauce over each. Makes 4 to 6 servings.

❦ Norwegian Meatballs ❦

"Norwegians like their meatballs tender—not like golf balls," says Verne Nels Osmundson. And for the life of us, we can't think of anything more that needs to be said about this excellent recipe.

> 1 pound each lean sirloin and lean pork, ground with a small piece of suet
> 3 thin slices day-old bread, crumbled
> 1 small onion, chopped
> 2 eggs, beaten
> 1 teaspoon salt
> 1 teaspoon cornstarch
>   Black pepper
> ¼ teaspoon allspice
> ¼ cup evaporated milk
> ¼ cup salad oil
>
> SAUCE
> 3 tablespoons flour
> 1 can (10½ oz.) beef bouillon
> 1 cup water
> 1 cup Burgundy

With a very, very light hand, using a fork so you don't crush the meat, mix meats, bread, onion, eggs, salt, cornstarch, allspice, pepper, and milk. Scoop up meat mixture with a round-bowled spoon; drop into oil heated in frying pan; turn to brown all sides. Remove meatballs to platter, and make sauce in same pan they were cooked in.

Stir flour into oil remaining in skillet and stir until it begins to brown. Add bouillon, water, and Burgundy slowly, stirring sauce until smooth and thickened. Place meatballs in sauce, cover, and simmer for 30 minutes. Chill in refrigerator overnight to set the flavors. Heat meatballs and serve on bed of noodles. Makes 6 to 8 servings.

⚜ Braised Tongue of Lamb ⚜

Willing to take a chance on something you have never tasted before? Let Samuel E. Vaughan be your trusty guide.

"Lambs' tongues are a part of the beast seldom mentioned in cookbooks, but for the small family for whom a large beef tongue is too much, they are just the thing.

"Here is a variant on a braised tongue recipe which is just about right for two hungry people or three dainty feeders."

> 6 lamb's tongues
> ⅛ teaspoon marjoram
> ⅛ teaspoon thyme
> ⅛ teaspoon basil
> ½ bay leaf
> 1½ cups water
> 1 carrot
> 1 medium-sized onion
> 2 stalks celery
> 2 pounds fresh mushrooms
> 2 tablespoons butter or cooking oil
> ¾ cup white wine
> 1 tablespoon flour
> ¼ teaspoon salt
> ½ teaspoon monosodium glutamate
> 1 teaspoon brown bottled gravy sauce
> 1½ teaspoons tarragon

Wash lambs' tongues in several waters. Place on rack in pressure cooker. Add a *bouquet garni* made up of the marjoram, thyme, basil, and bay leaf all tied up in a bit of cheesecloth. Add the 1½ cups water and cook 30 minutes at 15 pounds pressure. Save the liquor.

Meanwhile chop the carrot, onion, celery, and mushrooms. When tongues are cooked, remove skin and any small bones in the roots. Brown tongues well in the butter or oil in a heavy frying pan. Remove browned tongues to a 1-quart casserole. Place vegetables in the frying pan and gently cook until they are softened, but not fully cooked. Add the white wine and ¾ cup of tongue liquor into which you have mixed all the remaining ingredients. Bring this mixture to a boil and simmer a few minutes. Pour over the tongues and bake, uncovered, in a moderate oven (350°) for about 30 minutes. Makes 2 or 3 servings, depending on appetites.

DON'T LET ALL THOSE CLASSIC RECIPES SCARE YOU

Genealogy is diverting, but its ultimate discovery is the fact that all men are related. Much the same goes for the origins of recipes.

Suppose that you hungrily wish that you could devise a delectable dish. But you look at all those recipe books on the shelves. And you remember all the excellent dishes you have eaten in your time. And you ask yourself, "What chance have I to create something new, when people have been cooking for hundreds of years?"

Well, every normal hand has five fingers, yet policemen all over the world can pick out your fingerprints. Everyone has a voice, but those who know your voice don't mistake it. In all the arts, the artist makes some of his impact just from being an individual unlike any other. Good cooks cook with individuality, too, and you can learn to do likewise. There are "rules" of cooking that deserve to be obeyed, as experience gradually teaches you. But they have plenty of leeway for expressing your unique personality in the kitchen. So without fear or hesitation, go directly to the kitchen and prove that pudding.

Sweetbreads del Playa

"Try this in your experimental kitchen and see if it isn't good," says C. M. Simpson.

He deserves the first helping for his adventurous handling of sweetbreads, which is literally not everyone's dish. The addition of green peas gives color to something that is usually pretty monochromatic. It also offsets what one jesting tester calls "the cowardly texture of sweetbreads." For even more contrast, you might serve the mixture over something chewy—like toasted English muffins.

2 pounds sweetbreads
Water
1 tablespoon salt
1 pound mushrooms
¼ cup (½ cube) butter or margarine
½ cup chopped chives
¼ cup minced parsley or 2 tablespoons
dried parsley flakes
1 teaspoon salt
½ teaspoon pepper
¼ teaspoon oregano
Supreme Sauce (recipe follows)
1 package (10 oz.) frozen peas, cooked
Grated Parmesan cheese

Place sweetbreads in salted water to cover, and soak for 30 minutes; then simmer in same water for another 30 minutes. Drain, carefully remove membranes and dark parts from sweetbreads, cut into bite-sized pieces, and set aside.

Meanwhile cut up mushrooms and sauté in butter with chives and parsley, and season with salt, pepper, and oregano. Add this mixture to sweetbreads and place all in a greased casserole. Add Supreme Sauce and peas; mix thoroughly and sprinkle top with grated Parmesan cheese. Bake in moderate oven (350°) for 20 minutes. Serve with toasted garlic bread and a green salad. Makes 6 servings.

Supreme Sauce

In saucepan over medium heat, melt ½ cup butter or margarine. Blend in ½ cup flour, 1 teaspoon salt, ¼ teaspoon white pepper, and 1 teaspoon dry mustard. When thoroughly blended, add 3 cups chicken stock and stir with wire whisk until mixture thickens and comes to a bubbling boil. Remove from fire and add ¼ cup sherry.

Heretical Lamb Kidneys

It takes a good strong sauce to subdue lamb kidneys, in some people's opinion. Arnold Knight has the sauce, which he puts on while the kidneys are barbecuing. No reason why it wouldn't also make a good marinade. There is purposely a wide range of latitude in quantities of the ingredients that make the sauce penetrating and "hot."

It is quite possible that some may consider it heresy to cook kidneys so long, but try this recipe before you speak your mind.

12 lamb kidneys

SAUCE

2 cans (8 oz. each) tomato sauce,
diluted with 2 cans water
½ cup olive oil
2 to 4 cloves garlic, squeezed through press
6 to 10 sprigs fresh rosemary
1 teaspoon salt
1 teaspoon sugar
1 to 2 teaspoons chile powder
1 to 2 tablespoons Worcestershire
½ teaspoon pepper
French rolls or French bread

Split kidneys in half, remove and discard veins and fat, and soak overnight in salted water.

Combine all sauce ingredients and cook together about 20 minutes, until thickened a little.

Thread pieces of kidney on parallel skewers (for ease of turning over). Place on grill 7 to 9 inches above coals. Baste with sauce; turn every 5 minutes and baste each time they are turned. Kidneys should be done in 10 to 20 minutes.

Cut French rolls or French bread into thin slices, then into 2-inch squares. Be sure sauce is good and warm. Place piece of kidney between two bread squares and dip in sauce just before eating. (Napkins come in handy here.) Makes about 6 servings.

Wined Beef and Onions

William Tapia's recipe for wined beef is an elegant concoction that is reminiscent of the classic Boeuf Bourguignon. Mr. Tapia marinates his meat before cooking, and does the whole dish in an electric frying pan. The small onions are decorative as well as tasty.

2 pounds boneless round steak, ½ to ¾ inch thick
2 cloves garlic
¼ teaspoon oregano
½ teaspoon basil
¼ teaspoon pepper
2 tablespoons salad oil
Juice of 1 lemon
1 tablespoon bacon drippings
1 bay leaf
8 small white onions, peeled
1½ tablespoons capers
½ teaspoon Worcestershire
1 cup dry red wine
¾ teaspoon salt
1 tablespoon minced parsley

Cut the meat in strips 1 to 2 inches wide, crush garlic and spread over strips, then sprinkle with oregano, basil, and pepper. Sprinkle oil and lemon juice over beef and marinate 1 hour. Melt bacon drippings in an electric frying pan, and brown the beef pieces, then add bay leaf, whole onions, capers, Worcestershire, red wine, and salt. Reduce heat, cover, and simmer 30 to 40 minutes, or until beef is tender. Transfer to serving dish and sprinkle with minced parsley. Makes about 4 servings.

Veal Chops Francaise

Longtime chef Paul de Sainte Colombe likes to take a recipe from his native French cuisine and adapt it for preparation in an American kitchen.

4 tablespoons butter
6 veal chops, with all skin and fat removed
Salt and pepper
Pinch of tarragon
1 large onion, thinly sliced
1 cup shredded domestic Swiss cheese
½ cup cracker crumbs
½ cup white port
½ cup condensed beef consommé

On top of the range, in a frying pan that can also be put in the oven, melt 2 tablespoons butter and then lightly brown veal chops on both sides. Remove from heat, salt and pepper lightly, and add the tarragon. Cover each chop with slices of onion, cover the onions with Swiss cheese, and cover Swiss cheese with cracker crumbs. Put a small piece of butter on top of each chop. Pour the white port and the consommé into the pan and let this liquid spread around the chops. Cover, place in a moderate oven (350°), and cook about 45 minutes, until tender. Spoon extra liquid over chops. Makes 6 servings.

⟫⟫ Distinguished Liver and Onions ⟪⟪

Many enjoy eating liver and onions, but few consider it in any way a distinguished dish. The sauce doesn't make this look different from the usual liver and onions, but it does excellent things to the flavor. As Noel E. Damon explains, "The overall flavor of this simple entrée depends upon blending proper concentrations of the few ingredients, most important of which is a very rich brown stock. Short cuts or substitutes are universally disappointing."

You may find it advisable to make the stock at least a day ahead of time.

6 slices bacon
2 medium-sized onions, coarsely chopped
1 pound beef liver, in ¼ to ½-inch-thick slices
Flour
Salt and freshly ground black pepper
⅓ cup claret wine
⅔ cup brown stock (recipe follows)

BROWN STOCK

3 to 4 pounds beef shank bones
6 carrots
4 medium-sized onions
4 stalks celery
5 quarts water
2 cloves garlic
3 bay leaves
8 whole black peppers
1 teaspoon salt
1 teaspoon thyme
1 teaspoon basil
3 cups Burgundy wine

Cook bacon in large frying pan until crisp; remove, crumble, and set aside. Add onions to same pan, cooking slowly until tender; remove and set aside.

Roll liver in flour mixed with salt and pepper. Sauté liver quickly in the same pan over high heat, but taking care not to overcook and thereby toughen the meat.

When liver is still quite pink inside, add wine and de-glaze pan by stirring in all the brown bits stuck to it. Remove the pan from heat.

Add stock, crumbled bacon, onions, and a small additional amount of black pepper. Cover pan, return to low heat, and cook until sauce thickens, about 3 minutes. Slice liver into inch-wide strips, place in serving dish, and pour sauce over. (Or place atop a mound of buttered noodles and garnish with parsley.) Makes 3 to 4 servings.

Brown Stock

Place shank bones in a flat pan along with peeled carrots, quartered onions, and celery. Put under a broiler until bones become dark brown, turning once. Scrape all brown bits from pan as you transfer contents to a 6 to 8-quart kettle. Cover with the water. Add the garlic, bay, pepper, salt, spices, and wine, and simmer slowly for at least 6 hours, until total volume of liquid is reduced to 1½ to 2 quarts. During the first hour, stir the stock and skim off the foam. Do not stir stock at all thereafter.

Remove bones and strain liquid through several thicknesses of cheesecloth. Allow liquid to cool, uncovered, until fat solidifies on surface. Remove fat.

The stock can now be frozen; it keeps quite well—if it is well hidden from "the other cook."

A BIRD IN THE HAND

The celebrated French gastronome Brillat-Savarin held the firm belief "that the whole race of fowls was solely created to fill our larders and enrich our banquets. And certain it is that from quail to turkey-cock, wherever we meet with a member of this numerous family, we shall find food that is both light and savoury . . ."

For men cooks today, far and away the most important member of that race of fowls is the chicken. In recent years breeders have developed an extremely tender and lean type of broiler-fryer chicken, and poultrymen now raise it in stupendous quantity. It is very widely available and quite inexpensive.

Men cooks who know a good thing when they see one have applied themselves diligently to the problem of devising new ways to cook chicken. This chapter includes many recipes for chicken—cooked with gin, vermouth, limes, vinegar, prunes, and Chinese peas, not to mention more usual seasonings like wine and garlic. If you'd care to go further afield for fowl, there are also recipes here for pheasant, turkey, Cornish hen, duck, and dove.

Agreeable Barbecued Chicken

"We have fifteen grandchildren, all of whom like barbecued chicken drumsticks. Sometimes we have a lot of other chicken parts left over," says W. A. Leak in what may be a major understatement. And thereby hangs a recipe for barbecued chicken and dumplings.

"The exact spicing will depend upon how much they are smoked and how flavorful a barbecue sauce has been used. Our rotisserie-cooked chickens are lightly smoked and delicately flavored with an herb French dressing."

If you have this recipe in mind and want the barbecued flavor to be noticeable in it, give the chicken a pretty assertive marinade before it goes on the fire; then barbecue it good and smoky.

3 pounds barbecued chicken
2 stalks celery, sliced
2 medium-sized carrots, cut in large pieces
1 onion, diced
2 cloves garlic, finely sliced
Water
¼ cup sauterne
¼ cup dry sherry
1 teaspoon sage
¼ cup fresh parsley, minced
Salt and pepper to taste
Any leftover chicken gizzards, livers, or
hearts, boiled or barbecued separately
2 cups prepared biscuit mix
¾ cup milk

Cook chicken, celery, carrots, onions, and garlic together in water to cover, just until meat begins to come off bones. Remove bones. Add all remaining ingredients except biscuit mix and milk. Add more water if necessary to cover; bring to the simmering point. Combine biscuit mix and milk to make dumpling batter; drop by spoonfuls in simmering liquid and cook 10 minutes, uncovered. Cover and cook 10 minutes longer.

Makes 6 to 8 servings.

⑅ Soy-Broiled Winglets ⑅

John D. Steele's surgical know-how contributed greatly to the development of this ingenious recipe. After they are cut to his specifications, marinated, and then barbecued until dark brown, chicken wings become very respectable. As a matter of fact, they seem considerably more elegant than usual and look a little like tiny drumsticks.

Using available weapons, most chefs should be able to follow the directions for cutting. The important thing is to note how a chicken wing has three parts (possibly a startling resemblance to the human arm).

The marinade is simply soy sauce with any additions that appeal to you. You might try celery salt, garlic powder, and lemon juice to good effect.

To prepare the chicken wings, first use scissors to cut off the skin flap (dogs like this raw). Then take poultry shears or garden pruning shears and cut through lower end of the first part (corresponds to upper arm in human). Then cut through lower end of second or middle part (corresponds to human forearm) to finish cutting the wing into three parts. Discard third part.

On the other two parts of each wing, use a knife to push meat back ½ to ¾ inch from cut ends of bones. Marinate for 2 to 3 hours in soy sauce (with or without additional seasonings). Cook over coals until dark brown, turning occasionally with small tongs. Time will depend, of course, on heat of fire and distance from fire to grill, but should not exceed half an hour. These are also delicious cooked in a smoke oven.

⑅ Chicken Juniper ⑅

"It wasn't easy," says Pieter Kelder, "but I finally found a way that I like gin. A certain Russian restaurant served chicken cooked in gin, but naturally no recipe. So I researched, remodeled, and came up with this. I hope you find it as good as did those guests on whom I experimented."

In certain ways this dish may strike you as wasteful, but how gloriously so. By all means taste it before passing harsh judgment.

1 large broiler-fryer (about 4 lbs.),
cut in pieces, skin removed
½ cup dry sherry
½ cup honey
½ cup flour
½ cup (1 cube) butter or margarine
1½ cups gin
½ cup chopped parsley
½ cup chopped onion
½ teaspoon tarragon
2 tablespoons arrowroot or cornstarch
1 cup cream
Salt
Sesame seed

Rub chicken pieces with sherry and then with honey, or dip them in each. Dust lightly with flour and brown in butter. Arrange in buttered baking dish; pour over gin and sprinkle with parsley, onion, and tarragon. Bake in moderate oven (350°) for 1 hour. Remove chicken, keeping warm. To thicken sauce, blend arrowroot or cornstarch with about ½ cup liquid from the pan. Return to pan; add cream; cook, stirring until thickened. Salt to taste. Serve sauce over chicken and sprinkle with sesame seed. Makes 4 or 5 servings.

⚙ Smoke-Glazed Chicken ⚙

W. A. Leak advises that you cook this chicken in any smoke oven or in a regular barbecue with any sort of hood over the top (including one improvised of aluminum foil), to trap the smoke but keep it moving ever so slowly through the chimney. The important thing is to get the chicken well browned and thoroughly cooked.

1 fresh broiler-fryer (2 to 3 lbs.)
2 slices hickory-smoked bacon

For best flavor, use plump, unfrozen, local fryers. After washing and removing the giblets, place in smoke oven. Set a pan of hot coals, either charcoal or briquets (from hardwood only), about 8 inches below the fryer. Lay the 2 slices of high grade hickory-smoked bacon on top of the fryer. To make smoke, occasionally lay on the coals some small pieces of green spicy wood, preferably green apple wood, but green oak or grape is also good.

As the bacon melts, it absorbs smoke from the green wood and forms a glaze on the fryer. As soon as the chicken is rich brown on one side, turn it over and change the bacon again to the top side. About 1¼ hours in a light smoke, with the oven all but closed, produces a flavor quite distinct from anything else.

Salt and spices have purposely been omitted because little of either is needed and can be added according to personal preference. Makes 2 to 4 servings.

⚙ Harmonious Herb Chicken ⚙

"This dish is named for a pianist friend of mine, for whom it was first prepared," says Halsey Stevens. It incorporates a subtle and exceedingly harmonious combination of herbs and other seasonings.

1 teaspoon seasoned salt
⅛ teaspoon freshly ground black pepper
¼ teaspoon ground cardamom
¼ teaspoon dry mustard
½ teaspoon monosodium glutamate
2 plump broiler-fryers, cut in pieces
½ teaspoon tarragon
½ teaspoon rosemary
½ teaspoon sweet basil
½ cup dry sherry
¼ cup soy sauce
¼ cup lemon juice
2 tablespoons curaçao

Combine seasoned salt, pepper, cardamon, dry mustard, and monosodium glutamate; sprinkle evenly over chicken. Pound tarragon, rosemary, and basil in a mortar. Add to sherry, soy, lemon juice, and curaçao and pour over seasoned chicken. Marinate for 1 hour or longer. Remove chicken from marinade; place in roaster and bake, uncovered, in hot oven (400°) for about 1 hour, or until tender. Baste occasionally with marinade. Serve with steamed rice. Makes about 6 to 8 servings.

ꕔꕔ Chicken Cacciatore ꕔꕔ

Cacciatore is translated in an Italian dictionary as: "sportsman; light infantryman; groom who rides the royal carriage." As the word appears in Chicken Cacciatore, it would probably have to be translated into something like "chicken, hunter style." But it's interesting to speculate on how some infantryman might have snagged the original chicken, tomatoes, onions, and so on from a farmyard along the line of march, and then stewed them up at his leisure.

Tony Romano proposes a recipe for a winter cacciatore in which you get the essential tomato flavor from a can. It makes an appetizing dish, and the rich, red sauce will make you think of summer while the winter winds blow.

1 broiler-fryer (2½ lbs.), cut in pieces
Flour
3 tablespoons olive oil
3 tablespoons butter or margarine
1 medium-sized onion, chopped
½ pound mushrooms, sliced; or 1 can (6 or 8 oz.) whole button mushrooms, drained
2 teaspoons chopped parsley
1 clove garlic, minced or mashed
1 cup dry white wine
1 can (10¾ oz.) spaghetti sauce with mushrooms
2 bay leaves
½ teaspoon salt
⅛ teaspoon pepper
4 ounces spaghetti
Boiling salted water
2 tablespoons warm olive oil

Dredge the chicken pieces in flour to coat all over; sauté in the 3 tablespoons olive oil in a heavy frying pan until browned on all sides. Remove the chicken from pan and set aside. Add the butter to the pan and sauté the onion and mushrooms until lightly browned. Add the parsley, garlic, and wine; stir to scrape browned bits from bottom of pan. Return chicken to the pan; cover and simmer 10 minutes. Add spaghetti sauce, bay leaves, salt, and pepper. Cover and simmer for 45 minutes, or until tender. Remove bay leaves.

Meanwhile cook spaghetti in boiling salted water until just tender; drain and stir in the 2 tablespoons warm olive oil. Spoon the chicken and sauce over the top. Makes about 4 servings.

✵ Lime-Dill Chicken ✵

Always welcome are new ways to cook chicken. Enter and deliver chef Ed Colby.

1 small broiler-fryer (about 2 lbs.), halved
2 fresh limes
¼ cup (½ cube) butter
½ teaspoon chervil
¼ teaspoon onion powder
1 teaspoon ground dill weed
¼ cup sweet white wine
Salt and pepper to taste

Wash chicken and blot dry with paper towels. Place chicken halves in a baking dish and squeeze the juice of the limes over them; let stand for 1 hour, turning the halves once or twice.

While preheating the oven, make up a basting sauce by melting the butter and adding chervil, onion powder, dill, wine, and lime juice drained from chicken halves. Place the chicken halves on the broiler rack with the skin sides up; baste with part of the sauce and place under the broiler about 10 to 12 inches from the broiling element. Leave under broiler, basting frequently, until well browned.

Turn over the chicken halves and repeat the process. Total cooking time will vary from about 40 minutes to 1 hour, depending on the efficiency and construction of your oven. Season to taste and serve, spooning over chicken any basting sauce that remains in the pan. Makes 2 generous servings.

✵ Chicken Fry Babies ✵

When it's barbecue time and the wheel of choice is spun, it frequently comes up chicken. Virgil L. Newell gives the chicken a saucing and sizzling to remember.

1 cup vinegar
1 cup butter
¼ cup brown sugar
About 1 teaspoon celery seed, or to taste
1½ tablespoons Worcestershire
1 tablespoon hickory smoke salt
1 tablespoon monosodium glutamate
1 tablespoon onion salt
1 tablespoon coarse-ground pepper
2 broiler-fryers (about 2 lbs. each), halved

Combine all ingredients except chicken. Simmer together for 10 minutes to blend flavors. Wash chicken halves; then drain and pat dry. Coat with sauce and cook over a slow barbecue fire. Turn and brush the chicken halves with sauce mixture several times during cooking. Allow about 1 hour for cooking until done. Makes 4 servings.

❀ One-Dish Sunday Supper ❀

"This entrée was developed to fit the firm conviction at our house that Sunday is a take-it-easy day for the cook, when dinner should be prepared with minimum fuss and preparation time," tells Jerry Whalen.

His one-dish meal has a nice loose formula, allowing you to change vegetable ingredients and add seasonings just about as you please. The texture of the cooked vegetables is governed by the size of the pieces into which they are cut; chef Jerry likes his definitely on the crisp and chewy side to contrast with the rice. If you take it just as outlined here, the vegetables contribute most of the flavor and make it a rather mild dish.

2 tablespoons butter
1 small broiler-fryer
Salt
Pepper
Monosodium glutamate
1 small turnip
2 small carrots
2 green onions, with tops
1 medium-sized stalk of celery
½ slice bacon
1 small sprig parsley
1 cup packaged precooked rice
1 large ripe tomato
Lemon juice
Pinch of thyme

Melt the butter in a roasting pan. Dust broiler-fryer inside and out with salt, pepper, and monosodium glutamate. Peel turnip and scrub carrots. Cut onions, celery, carrots, and turnip into rather small bite-sized pieces; dice the ½ slice bacon; tear parsley sprig into coarse flowerets. Pile all vegetables and diced bacon loosely inside the chicken. Place chicken in roasting pan, breast side up. Roast in moderately hot oven (375°), uncovered, for approximately 1 hour, or until done according to your favorite test of tenderness. (If the vegetables are in large pieces, test them too.)

About 15 minutes before chicken is done, prepare rice according to package directions. Slice tomato and season lightly with lemon juice and thyme.

To serve, cut chicken in half and place a half on each plate. Toss the tender-crisp vegetables and some of the pan juices with the fluffy rice and serve onto plates. Garnish with tomato slices. Makes 2 servings.

⚒ Chicken in Vermouth ⚒

The Reverend Robert C. Hill ministers to the inner man in more ways than one; here he brings joy to the soul with Chicken in Vermouth.

1 broiler-fryer, cut in pieces
¼ cup flour, seasoned with salt and pepper to taste
1 clove garlic, halved
¼ cup salad oil
1 cup dry vermouth
6 small white onions
½ teaspoon basil
½ teaspoon rosemary
3 tablespoons chopped parsley
Water
2 teaspoons cornstarch
½ teaspoon salt
Pepper to taste
Pimiento (optional)

Shake chicken in flour and brown with garlic in oil. Remove garlic. Add vermouth, onions, basil, rosemary, and 2 tablespoons of the parsley. Cover and simmer about 1 hour, or until tender. Remove chicken from juice; adjust seasoning and thicken with cornstarch dissolved in a little water to make a gravy. Arrange chicken on platter, pour over a little gravy, and garnish with onions and pimiento, if desired. Sprinkle with the remaining parsley and serve.

Makes 4 servings.

⚒ Butter-Roasted Pheasant ⚒

"For years I experimented with pheasants," says Rawlins Coffman. "I cooked them in casseroles; I cooked them disjointed; I cooked them in wine; I tried all kinds of sauces and seasonings. The meat was invariably dry. Finally I found the answer—to my taste."

His method is simple, but he warns that it will not work "if the pheasant is so shot up or plucked as to have badly torn and broken skin."

1 pheasant
½ cup (1 cube) butter, melted

Carefully prepare the pheasant and wipe the carcass inside and out with a dry cloth. Put it on a roasting rack in an open roasting pan, breast down. Add no seasoning; simply cover the bird with a clean cotton cloth dampened thoroughly with melted butter. Place in a moderate oven (350°) and roast about 1 hour and 15 minutes, until the pheasant is done to your taste. Don't overcook this delicacy, since it should be a golden brown, juicy, and tender, ready to be served with your choice of delicate seasonings and sauces. Makes 2 or 3 servings, depending on the size of the pheasant.

ꙍ Rock Cornish Hen, Hunter Style ꙍ

The Rock Cornish game hen is about as domesticated as any other form of chicken, but its big advantage is small size—one to a person when you feel like eating heartily and leisurely. There's just enough resemblance to real game birds to justify Raymond E. Scott's naming of his recipe, "Rock Cornish Game Hen, Hunter Style." Says he, "It serves easily, is dainty in scale, attractive and elegant. Further, it has the advantage of keeping; thus it can be made early and kept in a warm oven, or even reheated."

The important thing is not to overcook these small birds. Once they pass the point of ideal tenderness, they very rapidly become too dry.

4 Rock Cornish game hens
About 1 teaspoon garlic powder
¼ cup olive oil
¼ cup melted butter
½ cup finely diced celery
½ cup finely diced carrots
1 medium-sized onion, chopped
2 cloves garlic, finely chopped
1 large can (1 lb., 12 oz.) plum tomatoes
1 green pepper, sliced in julienne strips about 1 inch long
1 large can (6 or 8 oz.) sliced mushrooms
¼ cup brandy
2 cups chicken stock or chicken broth
Salt and pepper to taste
¼ teaspoon oregano
⅛ teaspoon bouquet garni
3 tablespoons grated Romano cheese
1 cup fresh peas
1 tablespoon monosodium glutamate

Rinse hens in cold water; dry. Rub garlic powder on hens inside and out; set aside at room temperature for 30 minutes.

Place in a large chicken fryer with a heavy, tightly-fitting lid, and adequate depth to cover hens. Lightly brown hens on all sides in olive oil and butter. Remove from pan and add celery, carrots, onion, and garlic. Sauté until onion is transparent; do not brown. Drain tomatoes (reserve the liquor); dice the tomatoes and add with sliced peppers. Drain mushrooms and reserve liquor; add mushrooms to pan. Add brandy and stir. Sauté for 3 minutes. Add chicken stock, mushroom liquor, and tomato liquor. Salt and pepper to taste.

Arrange hens in pan; sprinkle with oregano and bouquet garni. Cover and simmer for 30 minutes, basting exposed surface of hens frequently (liquid should half cover them). Sprinkle with Romano cheese and add peas. Cover and cook just until tender, continuing to baste frequently. Sauce should be of medium consistency when finished. If too thin, remove hens to oven and reduce sauce as desired.

Immediately before serving, sprinkle with monosodium glutamate and stir in lightly. Place a spoonful of the sauce over each hen and send the balance of the sauce to the table separately. Serve with wild rice or pasta. Makes 4 servings.

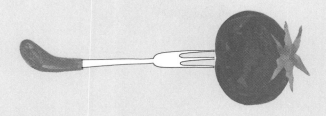

⚡ Supremes de Volaille ⚡

"I learned to read out of a cook book," says Dr. R. M. Hermes, "and have been collecting recipes ever since. I've had perhaps too much success at home, as my wife insists on my cooking dinner every day. She likes to shop and I don't, so we've worked out a kind of balance. She finds and I fix."

The success is not surprising if all of Dr. Hermes' dinners are as good as this dish of boned chicken breasts in cream. But, then, at an age when most of us were puzzling over "Run, Jip, run," he was getting stuck on the hard words like "marinate."

To accompany the chicken, you might serve fresh asparagus and dry white wine.

2 egg yolks
½ cup heavy cream
4 whole chicken breasts, boned, skinned, and halved (about 3 lbs. before boning)
½ lemon
⅓ cup flour
1 teaspoon salt
¼ teaspoon pepper
1 can (6 or 8 oz.) sliced mushrooms
1 tablespoon white wine vinegar
½ teaspoon freeze-dried chopped shallots
½ cup (1 cube) butter

Beat the egg yolks lightly with 2 tablespoons of the heavy cream. Rub the chicken breast pieces with the cut lemon, dip them in the yolk mixture, drain briefly, then dust them lightly in the flour that has been seasoned with the salt and pepper. Let stand on a rack for just about ½ hour, or leave it in refrigerator for up to several hours.

To the canned mushrooms and liquid, add the vinegar and chopped shallots. Heat the butter in a heavy frying pan until bubbly. Sauté the chicken breasts quickly until browned, about 2½ to 4 minutes a side, adjusting heat so butter does not burn.

Add the mushroom mixture; cover and cook for 3 minutes. Remove the chicken breasts to a heated platter and keep warm. Add remaining 6 tablespoons cream to remaining yolk mixture. Remove pan from heat and stir in yolk-cream mixture, scraping bottom and sides to remove browned bits. Stir over low heat until thickened, about 5 minutes on 300°. Pour over the breasts and serve. Makes 4 servings.

THE FIRST RECIPE

The first recipe to appear under *Sunset Magazine*'s column, "Chefs of the West"—way back in January of 1948—was an excursion on a recipe found in the old hand-written book of C. I. McReynolds' wife's mother. It is a classic of sorts, in that it set the tone for many good things that followed. The recipe is called Chicken in the Shell.

If you don't happen to have a supply of cockle shells in which to serve the chicken, it's just as good on toast rounds. The broth derived from simmering will make superlative soup.

1	(about 3-pounds) frying chicken, disjointed	1	tablespoon flour
1	onion, sliced	½	pint heavy cream
1	bay leaf	1	truffle, sliced
2	whole cloves	2	dozen mushrooms, chopped fine
1	blade mace		White pepper
6	whole peppercorns	2	egg yolks
1	tablespoon butter	2	tablespoons sherry

Place chicken, onion, bay leaf, cloves, mace, and peppercorns in a heavy stew pot. Cover with boiling salted water and simmer slowly for about 1 hour or longer, until chicken is tender. Set aside to cool. Remove meat from bones, discarding the skin. Cut meat into small dice.

Make Sauce: Melt butter in the top of the double boiler over low heat. Blend in flour, but do not allow to brown. Pour in cream gradually, stirring constantly to smooth, and add truffle, mushrooms, a dash of white pepper, then the diced chicken. Taste for salt content. Place over boiling water until quite hot. Add some of the hot sauce to beaten egg yolks, blending well. Return to sauce in double boiler, and cook 2 minutes longer. Blend in sherry and serve at once in cockle shells.

𝕎 Spit-Roasted Duck 𝕎

Most recipes for domestic duck try to accomplish two things to make the bird more palatable: reduce its content of fat, and introduce some sharp contrasting flavors. Michael Selvin accomplishes the first by spit-roasting, the second by a combination of five sweet or fruit-like ingredients that eventually form a thick glaze.

You can spit-roast the duck over a charcoal fire as well as in the oven. In either case, have a drip pan under it. Canned peach halves can be used when fresh peaches aren't available at the market.

2 canned peach halves, or 1 fresh peach
¼ cup brandy
½ cup soy sauce
2 teaspoons honey
1 orange, quartered
1 large domestic duck (3 to 4 lbs.)

Drain the canned peach halves (or peel the fresh peach and remove the pit). Mash the fruit, add brandy, and set aside for about 15 minutes or more before adding soy and honey to complete the basting sauce. Place the orange quarters inside the cavity of the duck and place it on the spit. Roast on the spit over a medium hot fire or in a 350° oven, basting quite often, for about 2 hours. Makes 4 servings.

⚜ Three-Dimensional Chicken ⚜

Landscape architect Robert Chittock likes to lay out a casserole dish three-dimensionally with layers of lasagne, chicken, cheese, and a white wine sauce. For further effect, he suggests serving it with a "tossed green fruit salad," containing one or more kinds of lettuce, mandarin orange sections, diced cucumber, chunks of pineapple, and an oil and vinegar dressing.

1 package (about 10 oz.) lasagne
Boiling salted water
½ pound fresh mushrooms
7 tablespoons butter
1¼ cups dry white wine
4 tablespoons flour
4 cups half-and-half (half milk, half cream)
1 teaspoon chopped fresh tarragon
(or ¼ teaspoon dried and crumbed tarragon)
Salt and pepper to taste
5 cups shredded, boned, cooked chicken
2 cups shredded Swiss, Gruyère, or jack cheese

Cook lasagne in boiling water until just tender, about 15 minutes; drain well.

Meanwhile, wash and slice the mushrooms; sauté in 3 tablespoons of the butter for about 3 minutes. Add 1 cup of the wine and allow to simmer until the wine is almost all evaporated; set aside.

Make a sauce by melting the remaining 4 tablespoons butter. Stir in the flour and cook until bubbly. Gradually stir in the half-and-half; cook, stirring, until thick and creamy. Add the mushrooms along with the remaining ¼ cup wine, the tarragon, and salt and pepper to taste. Simmer about 3 minutes longer.

In the bottom of a buttered, rectangular baking dish (about 9 by 13 inches), put a layer of the cooked lasagne and a layer of chicken; pour over some of the wine sauce; then sprinkle with some of the cheese. Repeat these layers several times, ending with a cheese layer. Bake in a moderate oven (350°) for about 40 minutes, or until bubbly and crusty on top. Makes about 8 servings.

⚜ Chicken Indonesia ⚜

Joseph Nolen presents this recipe which belongs in the company of worthy dishes. It is chicken gentled in a well flavored, fruity sauce.

1 large broiler-fryer
Cooking oil
1 onion, chopped
⅛ cup (¼ cube) butter
Water
1-inch cube fresh ginger, thinly sliced
1 tablespoon ground coriander
1 tablespoon chicken stock base
Salt   Pepper   Cayenne
Grated peel of ½ orange
1 teaspoon sugar
⅔ pint sour cream

Lightly brown chicken pieces in a little oil and set aside. In a large pan, sauté onion and butter until golden. Add chicken, enough hot water to cover it about two thirds, and chicken stock base, dissolved in some of the water. Let simmer for 15 minutes. Add ginger, coriander, salt, pepper, and cayenne to taste. Cook for another 40 minutes, adding more ginger and coriander toward the end, if you like. Add grated orange peel, sugar, and sour cream; cook until heated through. Serve over steamed rice. Makes 4 servings.

Viennese Pheasant Stuffing

You may note the Viennese influences in the stuffing ingredients and the seasonings for John Hughes' pheasant pièce de résistance.

1 large goose liver, or 2 chicken livers
¼ pound bulk pork sausage
4 tablespoons butter
Salt to taste
Freshly ground black pepper to taste
¼ teaspoon rosemary
2 or 3 lamb sweetbreads (or 1 veal sweetbread), parboiled 5 to 10 minutes and minced
1 tablespoon minced onion
3 or 4 tablespoons Madeira wine
1 large pheasant
2 tablespoons melted butter
Fresh vegetables, cooked, for garnish

Mince the liver, mix in the sausage meat, and brown in the 4 tablespoons butter, seasoning with salt, pepper, and rosemary as you do so. When this stuffing mixture is nearly cooked, add the minced cooked sweetbreads, minced onion, and Madeira wine. Cook 5 minutes longer, stirring to blend; then stuff the pheasant with this mixture. Roast the pheasant on a rack in an open roasting pan in a moderate oven (350°) for about 1½ hours, or until tender, basting frequently with the melted butter. Remove from oven and place on a platter; garnish with freshly cooked vegetables of your choice and serve. Makes 4 servings.

Ye Olde Domestic Duck

"This old duck recipe has made me a hero many times," modestly confesses A. L. Rodder. We assume "old" refers to "recipe." The grape flavor is excellent with duck, and the injection of Burgundy wine seems to make the meat especially tender and juicy, as well as adding unusually good flavor.

1 domestic duck (4 to 6 lbs.)
Salt and pepper
About 2 cups Emperor or Tokay grapes, seeded
About ¾ cup Burgundy wine
Garlic
Melted butter

The night before cooking, line the cavity of the duck generously with salt and pepper. Then stuff the cavity with grapes. Put duck in a pan. With a hypodermic needle (if you happen to have one available), or with a meat pump of the type used to inject liquid into pork when you're curing it, insert Burgundy wine into breast and legs. Rub meaty portions of duck with a cut clove of garlic; then paint all over with about 2 tablespoons melted butter. Place in refrigerator overnight.

The next day, place breast side up on a rack in a roasting pan and cook in a moderate oven (350°) for approximately 2 hours (or use your own judgment as to how well done you like duck). Baste occasionally.

To serve, cut down the center and then arrange so that one half has the grape-filled cavity facing up and the other facing down. You might serve with a trimming of parsley, some mint jelly, and rice or wild rice. Makes about 4 servings.

✗ Stuffed Chicken Thighs Kauai ✗

If the amount of chicken livers seems overstrong for your taste, it can be cut down without altering the essential character of Earl A. Knie's recipe. Incidentally, this is one of those three-part recipes consisting essentially of meat, marinade, and filling.

8 chicken thighs

MARINADE

¼ cup soy sauce
½ cup chicken broth
1 tablespoon honey
1 clove garlic, minced or mashed
1 teaspoon grated fresh ginger root
2 tablespoons Burgundy wine

STUFFING

1 cup chicken livers, cooked and mashed fine
2 tablespoons finely chopped dill pickles
2 tablespoons finely chopped green onions
2 tablespoons finely chopped green pepper
1 tablespoon chopped pimiento
⅛ teaspoon ground celery seed
⅛ teaspoon cayenne pepper

Flour
Salad oil or shortening
3 teaspoons cornstarch
1 tablespoon water

Bone chicken thighs; remove skin and gristle. Marinate about 30 minutes in a marinade of soy sauce, chicken broth, honey, garlic, ginger root, and wine. Meanwhile, combine all stuffing ingredients.

When chicken thighs have marinated, drain well, reserving marinade; then roll about a tablespoon of stuffing mixture into each. Fasten with skewers or string, roll in flour, and brown in hot shortening.

When they have become nicely browned, place in 1-quart shallow casserole. Add about ⅔ cup marinade; cover and bake 25 minutes in a moderate oven (375°). Mix together cornstarch and water; add remaining marinade and pour over chicken. Return chicken to oven uncovered and bake 15 minutes longer. Serve with steamed rice and a tossed green salad. Makes about 4 servings.

꧁ Turkey Elegante ꧂

After the brilliant first appearance of the turkey on the table, many cooks have discovered that leftover turkey meat is such a good and useful ingredient that it alone would justify the original roasting.

Says Robert W. McIntyre: "During those bygone days when life proceeded at a slower pace, we would often journey thirty dusty miles to spend Thanksgiving at our grandmother's house. These visits usually lasted a week, at least, and with the large amount of leftover turkey, grandma always had to find new ways to make this dish pleasing to our palates. One recipe proved to be a favorite time and time again."

2 packages (10 oz. each) frozen spinach
6 tablespoons butter or margarine
6 tablespoons flour
1½ teaspoons salt
Pepper to taste
3 cups milk
About 1 pound sliced turkey
⅓ cup grated Parmesan cheese
Toast points

Cook spinach as directed; drain thoroughly. Melt butter and blend in flour, salt, and pepper. Gradually add milk and stir constantly until thickened. In a greased baking dish, arrange a layer of spinach, then a layer of turkey, and finally the sauce. Sprinkle with cheese. Bake in a moderate oven (350°) for 15 to 20 minutes, or until all ingredients are heated through. Garnish with toast points. Makes 6 generous servings.

꧁ Risotto Rico ꧂

Halsey Stevens makes it quite clear: "This dish is frankly hybrid; it is a *risotto* that derives in some measure from a *paella*, but differs from both. While there are many dishes that combine rice and chicken, I have not encountered one that comes out quite like this."

If you're familiar with the lingo, you know that *risotto* is an Italian rice conglomeration; *paella* is a Spanish catch-all dish that frequently includes all kinds of fish and shellfish (in their shells); but when it is prepared away from the seacoast, chicken may be substituted. The saffron gives a strong yellow color, even in small amounts. The dish should appeal to those with reasonably sophisticated palates, especially if they favor saffron.

1 medium-sized onion, thinly sliced
¼ cup salad oil or butter
2 cups cooked chicken, removed from bones in largest pieces possible
¼ teaspoon saffron
3 cups chicken broth
Seasoned salt
Pepper
1 cup long-grain white rice, uncooked
½ cup grated Parmesan cheese

Brown onion slightly in oil or butter; add chicken and brown. Dissolve saffron in hot broth and add, along with seasoned salt and pepper to taste. Add rice and stir to level it. Cover and cook over low heat about 25 minutes, until broth is absorbed. Remove from heat, stir in grated cheese, and serve hot. Makes 8 servings.

❧ Breast of Pheasant ❧

"I do a lot of pheasant hunting, and once in a while a bird gets pretty badly shot up; that is how this recipe came to be developed," explains A. L. Rodder.

This recipe differs most from the usual in that you have to cut the breast off the bone. From there on, the procedure is simple and the meat is exceptionally well seasoned and flavorful.

1 large pheasant or 2 small pheasants
1 cup buttermilk
Salt to taste
Pepper to taste
Dash garlic salt
Pinch tarragon
½ cup fine dry bread crumbs
2 tablespoons butter
2 tablespoons salad oil
Half medium-sized onion, sliced
1 can (6 or 8 oz.) sliced mushrooms, including liquid

Cut breast meat off the breastbone of the pheasant and save the remainder of the pheasant for other use. Split breasts; marinate overnight in the buttermilk.

The next day, salt and pepper both sides and season with garlic salt and tarragon. Roll in bread crumbs.

Heat butter and oil in a heavy frying pan; add pheasant breasts and sliced onion; brown over medium heat for about 7½ minutes on each side. Reduce heat to low; add mushrooms, with their liquid. Cover and cook 5 minutes. Makes 2 or 3 servings.

❧ Chicken Livers Lorraine ❧

Charles C. Crockett savors this dish that satisfies the appetite at all hours of day or night. He had the courage to stick with a simple combination of seasonings. There's nothing cowardly about his Chicken Livers Lorraine. Men who like it (also some ladies) are apt to praise it extravagantly.

1 package (8 oz.) frozen chicken livers
¼ cup flour
Salt and pepper to taste
Butter
⅔ cup mayonnaise
2 tablespoons Worcestershire

Thaw chicken livers as directed on package. Coat generously with flour seasoned with salt and pepper. Sauté gently in butter for not more than 3 minutes on each side. Remove pan from heat and transfer chicken livers to warm serving dish. Mix mayonnaise and Worcestershire well; put this mixture in pan and scrape all bits of meat into it; then place it over chicken livers in serving dish and toss gently so all are coated. Put all in an oven that has been heated to 200° and then turned off. Keep in oven at least 15 minutes; flavor improves up to 45 minutes.

For breakfast or brunch, serve with scrambled eggs. For dinner, serve with egg noodles tossed with butter and sesame seed. Makes 4 to 6 servings.

⚛ Breast of Duck Marsala ⚛

Says R. L. Knighton: "This is primarily for all duck hunters who enjoy eating ducks as well as shooting them."

Marsala wine, which is used in the recipe, comes from a town of that name in Sicily. Some California wine is also marketed under that name, but probably more like the original is a California port.

> 4 duck breasts (8 pieces)
> 1 cup grated Parmesan cheese
> ¼ cup (½ cube) butter
> 1 cup sliced fresh mushrooms
> 1 teaspoon beef stock base or 1 bouillon cube
> ¼ cup Marsala wine

Cut the duck breasts in ⅜-inch slices and dredge in the Parmesan cheese. Sauté in ¼ cube of the butter for about 1 minute on each side. In a separate pan, cook the sliced fresh mushrooms in the remaining ¼ cube butter.

Remove duck from pan and place on heated platter. Arrange mushrooms over duck. Dissolve meat stock or bouillon cube in pan in which duck was cooked and add butter from pan in which mushrooms were cooked. Stir over low flame until well mixed. Add wine; heat and pour over meat and mushrooms. Serve immediately. Baked stuffed potatoes and a crisp salad go particularly well with this special dinner dish. Makes 4 servings.

⚛ Buttered–Barbecued Broilers ⚛

Carl W. Pearson has a baste for whole barbecued chicken. A nice tender young broiler slides off the spit pleasantly browned and properly juicy if painted with this potion. The onion and celery hidden away inside impart flavor in a very subtle way. Salt lovers might like a little more soy sauce in the basic mixture.

> 3 or 4 small onions
> 3 or 4 broiler-fryers (about 1½ to 2 lbs. each)
> 3 or 4 pieces celery
>
> BARBECUE SAUCE
>
> 1½ cups butter
> 1 teaspoon thyme, crushed
> ½ teaspoon oregano, crushed
> 1 clove garlic, crushed
> ¼ cup fresh lemon juice
> 1 teaspoon paprika
> 1 tablespoon soy sauce
> ½ teaspoon freshly ground black pepper, or to taste

Put one small onion and piece of celery in the cavity of each chicken. Tie wings and legs firmly. Impale birds securely on the spit crosswise, through the sides, alternating head to tail, tail to head. Barbecue 1½ to 2 hours over moderately hot coals, or until the skin is well browned and drumsticks move easily. Baste frequently with barbecue sauce, made as follows: Melt the butter in small saucepan; then add thyme, oregano, garlic, lemon juice, paprika, soy sauce, and pepper. Recipe makes 6 to 8 servings.

❧ **Eclectic Duck** ❧

"As the title indicates, I am not responsible for the genesis of this production," says Chester G. Brinck. "But after essaying numerous individual formulas, already in print, I have attempted to extract the best features of each and to combine them in a single operating procedure."

He recommends the same recipe also for Cornish game hens. You may or may not agree with him on this point, but there is no doubt that the rather sweet, spicy orange treatment is excellent for duck. If you use the domesticated variety, be sure to prick the skin all over with a fork several times during the cooking so the fat will drain out as it cooks.

1 domestic duck (4 to 6 lbs.), or 2 wild ducks
Salt and pepper
About 1½ tablespoons soft butter
1 teaspoon ground cloves
1 teaspoon cinnamon
1 teaspoon ginger
1 teaspoon nutmeg

SAUCE

2 large oranges
2 tablespoons sugar
2 teaspoons arrowroot or 1 tablespoon cornstarch
3 tablespoons hot duck drippings
1½ ounces (3 tablespoons) Cointreau,
Curaçao, or Grand Marnier
Salt to taste

Rub duck all over with salt and pepper, then with the soft butter. Anoint well inside and out with the *quatre épices*—clove, cinnamon, ginger, nutmeg. Place duck, breast side up, on a rack in a shallow pan. Roast in a moderate oven (350°) for about 2 hours, or until tender (check wild ducks after 1 hour). Baste occasionally with pan drippings.

To make the sauce, cut the outer zest (peel) off ½ orange with a vegetable peeler, cut into slivers, and drop into boiling water for about 2 minutes; drain and set peel aside. Ream the orange and set juice aside. Combine sugar, arrowroot, and the 3 tablespoons hot duck drippings. Stir in the orange juice and peel, and bring to a boil, stirring. Continue boiling until correct viscosity has been achieved (should be fairly thick); then add the liqueur and salt to taste. Remove from heat. Ladle sauce generously over duck before serving. Makes 2 to 4 servings.

⋙ Week-Enders Chicken ⋘

"It seems that my pad is the congregating spot for a group of people on Sunday afternoons," says bachelor Ron Reeves. "The varied activities often include my cooking."

Ron has the right instincts, for he has kept effort to the minimum necessary to give this chicken dish the maximum effect of luxuriousness, the better to entertain and please his guests.

Salad oil or shortening
2 or 3 cloves garlic, cut in half
About ¾ cup grated Parmesan cheese
1 teaspoon salt
¼ teaspoon pepper
½ teaspoon sage
1 large broiler-fryer (about 3 lbs.), cut in pieces
1 egg, beaten
1 tablespoon water
1 cup commercial sour cream
½ cup slivered almonds
1 tablespoon sesame seed

Heat oil in a frying pan and place garlic cloves in it while it's heating. Combine the cheese with salt, pepper, and sage. Dip chicken in egg beaten with water, and roll in cheese mixture. Remove garlic cloves from pan and discard. Cook chicken on moderately high heat 15 minutes, or until cheese coating has browned.

Remove chicken from frying pan and place in an open baking pan. Roast, uncovered, in a moderate oven (350°) for 30 minutes. Remove chicken from oven, pour sour cream over it, and sprinkle slivered almonds and sesame seed on top. Slip the pan under the broiler just long enough to toast the nuts and seeds. Makes 4 servings.

If there is some chicken left over (which is rare), wrap the individual servings in foil, along with some of the sour cream, and freeze. To serve, just put in a moderate oven (350°), still sealed, and bake about 45 minutes. Often it tastes better than original batch.

Doves San Joaquin

"The great San Joaquin Valley is famous for its many fine and productive vineyards; however, to many nimrods, it is no less well known for its fine dove shooting each September," relates Sidney W. Newell. "It seems logical and almost inevitable that these two great and simultaneously harvested crops be combined to make Doves San Joaquin."

The juice of the grape—made into claret—also helps blend such diverse ingredients as carrots and mushrooms into a harmonious whole. For a more fruity and exotic flavor, you might try fewer carrots and more grapes. Make the recipe with Cornish game hens if you have no doves.

3 or 4 slices bacon
10 doves, dressed and wet from washing
Flour
Salt
Pepper
1 cup consommé
1 cup claret wine
1 stalk celery
3 carrots, thinly sliced
½ cup fresh mushrooms, chopped
1 cup seedless grapes (or raisins may be substituted)
½ cup orange juice

Fry bacon until about half cooked; remove bacon, saving the drippings. Dredge doves in flour seasoned with salt and pepper; then sauté in bacon drippings. Arrange doves in frying pan or casserole with small piece of bacon across the upturned breast of each. Add consommé, claret, celery, and carrots.

Cover and either simmer slowly or bake in a moderate oven (350°) for 30 minutes. Add mushrooms and grapes; cover again and cook an additional 15 minutes. Add orange juice; cover or not as desired and cook for a final 15 minutes, or until meat begins to loosen from the bones. Remove birds and discard celery. Adjust gravy by adding water to thin, or by cooking with cover removed to thicken. Makes 4 servings.

⚛ Pheasant Paisano ⚛

Here's a pheasant recipe based on one bird for each lucky guest. It comes from a veteran experimenter, Charles L. Palmer, of Fresno, California, who doesn't mind volunteering that squab is a quite acceptable substitute for pheasant in this recipe.

1 stalk celery
¼ teaspoon rubbed sage
¼ package dried onion soup mix
1 pheasant (or squab), dressed
1 slice bacon

SAUCE

Drippings
¼ cup white or red wine
1 teaspoon lemon juice
1 small can (3 oz.) sliced broiled mushrooms
Salt to taste
1 slice toast
Bacon and parsley for garnish

Cut celery stalk to fit into cavity of bird and place sage in channel of stalk, taking care not to spill. Spread out a piece of foil big enough to cover the bird and put onion soup mix in center. Place bird on top, with slices of bacon over breast. Do not salt or pepper. Wrap tightly and put in oven (375°) for 30 to 35 minutes.

Remove bird from foil (save drippings); set bacon aside, discard celery, and put bird in a broiler pan.

Combine drippings, wine, and lemon juice in saucepan and reduce slightly. Place bird under broiler for 5 minutes, or until brown (do not dry out). Meanwhile, add mushrooms (including the liquid in the can) to sauce and continue to cook it in saucepan (while the bird browns) until it has become slightly thick. Salt to taste.

Place slice of toast on plate and cover with sauce. Then place bird on toast; garnish with bacon and parsley, and serve.

FOR FISH FANCIERS

Men like to catch fish, so you will often find them taking the responsibility for cooking it simply because they don't like to have it all presented to the cat. As they get more expert, they develop firm convictions, even passionate prejudices, about the proper way that fish should be cooked.

In the recipes that follow, you will notice a great deal of attention given to exact timing, for fish flesh is one of the most delicate of foodstuffs that we subject to the cooking process.

Shrimp is the form of fish that appears often in these recipes, closely followed by crab. Both of these are shellfish, plentiful and of good quality along the Pacific Coast. Both go well in combination with other fish. There are also prized recipes here for salmon, rockfish, sole; and—going more particularly into Pacific specialties—abalone and mahimahi.

◈ Marinated Mahimahi Fillet ◈

For some years, West Coast markets have carried a white fish of delicate texture and mild flavor, caught and frozen in the Hawaiian Islands. As Clifford Roehr points out: "Actually the mahimahi (pronounced ma-hee ma-hee) is a common dolphinfish (not to be confused with the seagoing mammal called the dolphin) and is found off both coasts of the American continent."

However, credit goes to the Islanders for making it so widely available and blessing it with their musical name. Clifford Roehr goes along with the Hawaiian spirit of things in his invention of this simple and very good recipe.

1 cup canned papaya juice
½ cup light cream
Juice of 1 lemon
1 teaspoon salt
1 teaspoon monosodium glutamate
1 teaspoon Worcestershire
2 pounds mahimahi fillets
Flour
Butter (about ¼ cup or ½ cube)
Lemon wedges
Parsley

To make marinade, combine papaya juice, cream, lemon juice, salt, monosodium glutamate, and Worcestershire. Cut fillets into serving-sized pieces, and marinate for about 30 minutes. Remove from marinade, dip fillets in flour to coat both sides, and sauté quickly in butter for about 5 minutes, or just until golden brown on both sides and you can flake it with a fork. Remove to hot platter, cover with the browned butter from the pan, and garnish with lemon wedges and parsley. Makes 4 servings.

◈ Fish Fillets Superb ◈

Here is one of the best things that ever happened to sole, although almost any other type of fish fillet or fish stick could hardly miss in this superb recipe from Richard C. Alcorn. The sauce is sharp flavored and creamy.

2 pounds sole, rockfish, or other fish fillets
Cooking oil
1 can (10 ¾ oz.) cream of mushroom soup
2 tablespoons dry sherry
1 tablespoon capers
½ teaspoon Worcestershire
1 cup grated Cheddar cheese
Paprika

Brush fish with oil and put under the broiler—not too long (8 to 10 minutes for sole fillets), for the next step continues the cooking. Meanwhile mix soup, sherry, Worcestershire, and capers to make sauce.

Transfer fish to metal steak platters, or any shallow, heat-resistant pan or platter. Spoon sauce over fish, sprinkle with the grated cheese, and top with a dash of paprika. Place under the broiler again until cheese is nice and bubbly, but not too brown. Serve hot. Makes 4 servings.

✂ Fillets de Sole sans l'Eau ✂

"It is my firm conviction that sole should never be touched with water, fumet, court bouillon, or any other aqueous concoction," states Laurence Berlowitz. "The poaching of sole dilutes and destroys a delicate and distinctive flavor, somewhat reminiscent of old dry sherry, but quite undefinable. Less harmfully one may coat the fillets in a mixture of masa (cornmeal flour) and unbleached flour and then fry them.

"The best procedure, however, is to immerse the fillets nude in melted butter and brown lightly on both sides. This process brings out all the flavor, glazing the sweetness of the exterior of the fish."

1 to 1½ pounds sole fillets
Soy sauce
Pepper
¼ cup (½ cube) butter
2 bunches spinach (about 2 lbs.), steamed in butter
1 teaspoon lemon juice
Mornay Sauce (recipe follows)
4 medium-sized potatoes, boiled whole and chilled
Butter or salad oil
Ground cloves
4 carrots, boiled whole

MORNAY SAUCE

½ medium-sized onion, chopped
¾ cup dry white wine (preferably same as you will drink with the meal)
1 cup Bechamel or white sauce
¼ cup grated Parmesan cheese
¼ cup shredded Gruyère cheese
2 tablespoons carrot purée

As soon as possible after purchase, coat sole fillets with a light coating of soy and pepper. Melt the ½ cube butter in large frying pan until bubbly; cook fillets over medium heat until lightly browned, turning once very carefully to brown the other side (about 4 minutes on a side).

On a flat, oven-proof platter, spread out the butter-steamed spinach in a layer. (To butter-steam, use about 2 tablespoons butter.) Sprinkle lemon juice over, then arrange browned fillets on top and cover with Mornay Sauce (recipe follows).

Cut potatoes into thin slices and brown in butter or oil, sprinkling over them a very small amount of ground cloves as they brown. Arrange potato slices in a border around the fish. On top of Mornay Sauce, arrange carrots, whole or cut into shorter lengths. Place platter in a hot oven (400°) for a short time until Mornay Sauce is browned. Makes 4 servings.

The wine of preference for this meal: Folle Blanche or an extremely dry sherry.

Mornay Sauce

Boil chopped onion in wine for 10 minutes. Add onion-wine fumet to Bechamel sauce and boil down, stirring constantly, until reduced by one third. Add the two cheeses and carrot purée. Strain or blend smooth. The final sauce should be quite thick.

ꔛ **Rockfish with Avocado** ꔛ

Richard C. Alcorn has the touch when it comes to fish dishes. Here's an important footnote: Slice the avocado nice and thin, then do a neat job of overlapping the slices on top of the fish to form a kind of frosting over it.

3 pounds rockfish fillets
1 can (12½ oz.) evaporated milk
⅓ cup flour
⅔ cup fine dry bread crumbs
1 teaspoon salt
¼ teaspoon pepper
¼ cup salad oil
2 avocados
½ cup lemon juice
⅓ cup chopped parsley

Dip fish in evaporated milk and dredge in mixture of flour, bread crumbs, salt, and pepper. Cook quickly in oil until nice and brown, but juicy inside. Overlap thin slices of ripe avocado on top, sprinkle with lemon juice, and top with parsley. Makes 10 to 12 servings.

ꔛ **Snapper in "Champagne" Sauce** ꔛ

Joseph Nolen's travels in many countries have acquainted him with the foods of many nationalities. The following dish has a flavor much like that of a French champagne sauce, but there's not a drop of champagne in it. The secret is the use of a blender, which alters the flavors of the original inexpensive ingredients.

4 rockfish fillets, or other white fish
Limes or lemons
1 medium-sized onion
1 tomato
1 green pepper
2 tablespoons butter
1½ cups hot water
½ cup commercial sour cream
1 teaspoon fresh tarragon leaves
1 small clove garlic
1 tablespoon chicken stock base
Salt to taste
Pepper to taste
Cayenne to taste
32 capers

Lay fillets in flat dish and squeeze lime (preferred) or lemon juice over them. Let sit for 1 hour. Meanwhile, sauté chopped onion, tomato, and green pepper in butter for 5 minutes. Add all remaining ingredients except capers. Simmer 15 minutes, put through blender (or sieve), return to pan, and simmer 5 minutes more. Put fillets in individual heavy foil pieces and add sauce and 8 capers to each package. Seal foil package and bake at 350° for 45 minutes. Remove from foil and serve immediately. Makes 4 servings.

⚒ Shrimp with Real Sole ⚒

Something about eating fish and shellfish together makes one feel doubly fortunate. Sole and shrimp are each fine in their own way; but both—what riches!

B. A. Getschmann has put in certain touches of elegance: parsley, dill, egg in two forms, and capers; however, experimenters might try one more discreet addition of a favorite herb or other seasoning.

Warning: Don't overcook the fish. The thin fillets should not be cooked so long that their texture becomes crumbly.

> 1 tablespoon butter or margarine
> 1 small onion, minced
> ½ cup soft bread crumbs
> Milk
> 15 cooked shrimp (about ½ lb.), finely minced
> ½ teaspoon chopped parsley
> ⅛ teaspoon powdered dill or ¼ teaspoon dill weed
> 1 hard-cooked egg, mashed fine
> ½ teaspoon salt
> Pepper to taste
> 1 egg white, beaten stiff
> 6 fillets of sole, each approximately same size
> Egg sauce (recipe follows)

Melt butter in a saucepan and add onion. Stir for a moment but do not brown. Add bread crumbs (previously soaked in as much milk as they will absorb, but with superfluous milk squeezed out just before you use them). Add shrimp, parsley, dill, egg, salt, and pepper. Cook gently for 3 minutes. Add egg white, beaten stiff, and fold in. Remove from heat.

Fill fillets of sole with shrimp mixture. Roll and fasten with toothpicks. Arrange in a greased shallow baking pan. Bake in moderate oven (350°) for 20 minutes, or just until sole flakes with a fork. Remove toothpicks, serve with Egg Sauce. Makes 6 servings.

Egg Sauce

Melt 2 tablespoons butter or margarine in saucepan. Add 2 tablespoons flour, ¼ teaspoon salt, and ¼ teaspoon white pepper; stir until smooth. Whipping with a wire whisk, add ½ cup consommé diluted with ½ cup dry white wine. Simmer 5 minutes. Add 3 hard-cooked eggs, chopped fine, and 2 tablespoons heavy cream. Heat *but do not boil*. Remove from heat; add 1 teaspoon Worcestershire, 1 teaspoon chopped parsley, 1 teaspoon capers.

Serve hot over fillet of sole rolls.

⨽ Pickled Salmon Belly ⨽

There's nothing primitive about Alfred Lindahn's recipe for salmon belly. Taste the results, and note the simplicity of preparation. The morsels are "delicious with rye bread and beer; good for appetizers, snacks, or little sandwiches."

2 pounds salmon bellies
¼ cup salt
1 quart white vinegar
2 teaspoons sugar
2 teaspoons mixed pickling spices
2 teaspoons tarragon
2 teaspoons thyme
½ bay leaf, crumbled

Salt the salmon generously; let stand with salt about 48 hours, then rinse well under cold water. Simmer for 10 minutes with vinegar. Cut into 1½-inch cubes. In a quart jar or refrigerator container, layer the salmon cubes with a combination of the sugar, pickling spices, tarragon, thyme, and bay leaf. Pour over cooled vinegar; cover tightly. Keep in refrigerator; three weeks later it's ready to eat.

To serve, rinse salmon cubes in cold water to wash off spices. Remove bones, scrape off skin (don't cut it off), and cut meat into thin slices. Two pounds of salmon bellies make about 1 quart.

⨽ Bubbling Crab Casserole ⨽

Asparagus is extremely compatible with other foods, as Dr. Robert Dyar proves by combining it successfully with a rich mixture of other casserole ingredients. You could cut back on either the cheese or the almonds and still have a very satisfying dish, but you may find occasion to increase the wine a little.

1 cup spaghetti, uncooked
Salted water
1 cup thick cream sauce
1 cup shredded mild Cheddar cheese
⅛ teaspoon dry mustard
⅛ teaspoon paprika
½ cup dry white wine
1 cup cooked asparagus tips
1 pound fresh crab meat
½ cup chopped toasted almonds

Break spaghetti into 2-inch pieces; cook in salted water until barely tender. Heat cream sauce and add grated cheese, mustard, and paprika. When cheese is melted, stir in wine. Cover the bottom of a greased 1-quart casserole with a little of the sauce. Add half the cooked spaghetti in a thin layer, then a layer of asparagus and a layer of crab. Cover with about half the remaining sauce and add a few chopped almonds.

Then repeat layers of spaghetti, asparagus, and crab; pour on remaining sauce; and top with remaining toasted almonds.

Set casserole in a shallow pan of hot water. Place in a moderately slow oven (325°) and bake approximately 30 minutes, or until hot and bubbling.

Serve with green salad, French bread, and white wine. Makes 4 to 6 servings.

⚛ Marinated Cracked Crab ⚛

E. Jeff Barnette, an inveterate experimenter, turns his attention to cracked crab. He marinates it, so the result is a little juicy for eating out of hand. But the flavor is excellent. Try it for a patio meal; and if you want to be even more thoughtful, furnish each diner a towel that has been immersed in hot water and then squeezed until it is just barely too dry to drip.

3 freshly cooked crabs (about 2 lbs.) each
3 tablespoons wine vinegar
6 tablespoons olive oil or other salad oil
3 tablespoons chopped parsley
3 small cloves garlic, crushed
1 teaspoon salt
Dash freshly ground pepper

Scrub, drain, and crack crab. Mix other ingredients together; pour over crab and refrigerate for 15 minutes (covered). Stir twice while refrigerated, making sure all is thoroughly marinated. Makes 3 or 4 servings.

⚛ Crab-Rice-Cheese Bake ⚛

In about one hour from start to finish, Thomas H. Swindoll can have this crab, rice, and cheese casserole ready to serve.

It needs no more seasoning than wine, but it is the type of dish that is quite receptive to other subtle additions—almost any that are compatible with shellfish and cheese. If you want to make it really luxurious, you could increase the amount of crab.

½ teaspoon salt
3 cups water
1½ cups uncooked rice
2 eggs
4 tablespoons butter
3 tablespoons flour
1 cup milk
1 cup shredded Cheddar cheese
½ cup sherry or dry white wine
½ pound (or more) crab meat
Pepper
Shredded Cheddar cheese
Pimiento strips (optional)

Bring salted water to a boil in a heavy pot with lid. Add rice, cover, decrease heat, and steam for 15 minutes. (Do not uncover during cooking!)

Meanwhile hard-cook the eggs, and prepare a cheese sauce as follows:

Melt butter in a saucepan, stir in the flour. Gradually add milk and cook while stirring with a whisk until mixture is thick. Add the 1 cup cheese and stir until cheese is melted. Taste and add more salt if needed (also pepper and other seasoning, if desired). Remove from heat and stir in wine.

Dice the hard-cooked eggs. Combine rice, sauce, diced eggs, and crab meat. Place in a buttered casserole dish (about 2-quart size) and cover with a little more shredded Cheddar cheese. Decorate top with pimiento strips. Bake 30 minutes in a moderate oven (350°). You can cook longer if you prefer a more crusty effect. Makes 4 to 6 servings.

⚒ Charcoal Broiled Prawns ⚒

When the critical crowd gathers on the patio, wondering, "What will he bring forth now?" it's good to have a ready answer.

It is supplied by Edward P. Colby. His delectable prawn bits make excellent hors d'oeuvres for eating on the hoof, but none will spurn them if served at the table as an entrée. There's that touch of smoke in the flavor that appeals to most connnoisseurs of barbecued food.

6 large prawns, fresh or frozen
½ cup (1 cube) butter or margarine
2 tablespoons olive oil
2 tablespoons steak sauce
6 crushed garlic cloves
1 teaspoon crushed basil
1 teaspoon crushed tarragon
1 teaspoon crushed celery seeds
2 tablespoons dry white wine
Salt to taste

Shell and devein the prawns and split each in butterfly fashion. (Cut down back side almost all the way through so prawn will lay out flat; take care not to cut entirely in half.) Combine all other ingredients except salt in a sauce. Marinate prawns in the sauce at least 1 hour. When coals in the barbecue have reached the glowing stage, spread tails out on the grill, turning them and basting often. When they show a little brown color, salt to taste, remove from fire, cut into 1-inch pieces, and serve immediately. Makes about 6 servings for hors d'oeuvres, 2 as an entrée.

There are worse dishes, but few better.

⚒ Salmon Vinifera ⚒

L. J. Lessard barbecues salmon slices between grape leaves:

"*Fresh* salmon is of utmost importance. If you are a fisherman and catch your own, you must keep it fresh until cooked . . . Build a barbecue fire from charcoal, oak bark, or any other non-resinous wood. When the coals are gray and there is no flame, the heat will be correct for cooking salmon . . . During the cooking, green oak leaves may be put on the fire to give a smokier flavor, if desired . . . Fresh grape leaves are available for many months of the year; when they are not, preserved grape leaves may be used." The grape leaves protect the salmon from scorching and drying out and keep the meat tender and very moist. The method should work equally well for steelhead.

Slice the salmon down each side, removing the bone. (If you purchase salmon at a market, this will be done for you and the two long slices will be labeled "fillets.") If the salmon is large, cut off the salmon belly, which is thin, and discard it. Then cut in fairly small pieces as uniform in thickness as possible so one portion will not be overcooked while another is undercooked. Sprinkle with garlic salt.

Place each piece, skin down, on a slightly larger grape leaf. Put on rack or grill over barbecue fire, leaving a little space between leaves. Cook for about 10 minutes. Then place another grape leaf over the top of each piece, turn over, and cook approximately 10 minutes more, until salmon is cooked through but not cooked dry. Remove from grill and serve with green salad and sourdough French bread.

⚞ **Appetite-Appeal Abalone** ⚟

"Being a skin diver, I have come to appreciate abalone as one of the finer things of living in California," relates Louis A. Messer. "However, as much as I like to eat them, abalone are time consuming and messy to prepare. One day I was too hungry and tired from the swim to pound them. A bit of empirical design based around what I found in the cupboard yielded the following."

Skin divers, and others, who don't catch abalone, take heart. This recipe can do equal wonders for clams (particularly the tough necks), mussels, or anything else of comparable consistency. The hors d'oeuvre version is probably best, followed by patties, and then sandwiches.

2 average-sized, very fresh green or pink abalone
1¼ cups crumbled graham cracker pieces
6 large, ripe, pitted olives
1 medium-sized sweet onion
1 tablespoon prepared mustard
2 tablespoons dried parsley flakes
2 eggs
2 tablespoons lemon juice
½ teaspoon salt
½ teaspoon seasoning salt
¼ teaspoon black pepper
2 slices bacon
Butter

It is important that the abalone be shucked when fresh. Even though they will keep more than a day in the refrigerator, each abalone so stored will lose over half a cup of "milk." Besides the mess, you lose much of the delicate flavor unique to abalone. If you are in a hurry to store abalone for future use, shuck them, discard the intestine, and freeze the entire muscle immediately. The unwanted darker portions of the foot may be trimmed off after it is thawed for use.

Probably one of the commonest mistakes made in preparing abalone is to attempt to salvage too much meat. Slice off all the circumferential fringe flesh and the brown skin, even if some white meat is lost (after all, the law allows you five per day). The exact amount to trim off the foot depends upon size. Larger specimens have a thicker layer of dark meat. This should all be donated to the cat, who will enjoy it much more than your guests, since it has a strong flavor.

Once the muscle is trimmed down to the edible portion, pass abalone, crackers, olives, and onion through a food chopper. Do not bother to pound the "ab" first. Retrieve all juice. Mix in mustard, parsley, eggs, lemon juice, salts, and pepper. Cook the bacon until limp and pass it through the chopper. Add the bacon and fat to abalone and mix thoroughly.

The best method of cooking is to roll the mixture into one-inch balls and pan-fry in an electric frying pan in a small amount of butter. Fry 3 minutes at 300°, turning frequently. Abalone, like liver, must not be overcooked. Serve from a chafing dish as hors d'oeuvres. Your guests will never be able to guess what they were served, but your chafing dish will be empty. Makes about 60 hors d'oeuvres.

Variation 1

Make patties. Dot with butter and broil about 3 inches below heat for about 2 minutes on each side. Use a sheet of foil over the broiler pan. Makes 12 lunch-sized patties.

Variation 2

Reduce cracker crumbs to ¾ cup and use mixture as sandwich filler between a slice of wheat and a slice of oatmeal bread. Butter the outside of each slice and place the sandwich in a sandwich grill; grill until well toasted on each side. Makes 12 sandwiches.

San Francisco Seafood Bake

Daryl Hopkins passes on a treasured recipe for seafood which he "evolved after forty years of cooking and eating in and around San Francisco."

This combination of white fish, shellfish, cheese, and white sauce all bubbling in a casserole is a minor classic in various San Francisco seafood restaurants. But there are various way to achieve it, and here is a good one. If you'd rather not use canned white sauce, by all means make your own more distinguished alternative.

Hopkins thoughtfully adds, "Amounts are given for two servings. I'd rather build up from two than tear down from six; and besides, good recipes for two are hard to come by."

¾ cup cooked crab meat
¾ cup cooked and shelled small shrimp
2 tablespoons shredded sharp Cheddar cheese
2 medium-sized fillets of sole, split in
half down center line
White Sauce (recipe follows)
1 tablespoon shredded Parmesan cheese
1 tablespoon chopped parsley

WHITE SAUCE

2 tablespoons finely chopped onion
2 tablespoons finely chopped celery
2 tablespoons butter
Dash of garlic powder
⅓ cup white wine or light sherry
1 can (10½ oz.) white sauce

Lightly butter two oval 9-inch casseroles. Toss crab and shrimp with Cheddar cheese and mound half the mixture the long way down the center of each casserole. Place one split half fillet of sole on each side of the mounds and gently press down to mold and firm the mixture.

Cover with warm white sauce; sprinkle with Parmesan cheese and parsley. Place in moderately slow oven (325°) for 20 minutes, or until sauce is bubbling and slightly brown. Makes 2 servings. Accompany with sourdough French bread, tossed green salad, and a well chilled bottle of white wine.

White Sauce

In top of double boiler, sauté onion and celery in butter until wilted, not browned. Add garlic powder and wine. Cook down until reduced by about half, then add canned white sauce, stir until there are no lumps, and keep warm and covered in double broiler until ready to use.

❦ Clock Watcher's Shrimp ❦

The shrimp is one of those foodstuffs that can go from underdone to overdone in a matter of seconds. So keep your trusty timer handy when you try this recipe submitted by William Tapia. Try it with rice for a Sunday night supper.

2½ pounds large fresh or frozen shrimp
6 tablespoons butter
Salt
2 tablespoons lemon juice
¾ cup dry white wine
¾ cup water
1 bay leaf
1 slice onion
6 whole black peppers
3 tablespoons flour
½ cup heavy cream
5 tablespoons grated Romano cheese

Shell and devein raw shrimp. Melt 1 tablespoon of the butter in frying pan; lay shrimp in it, salt lightly, and sprinkle with lemon juice. Pour wine and water over; add bay leaf, onion, and pepper. Cover and simmer for 3 minutes; strain and reserve liquid. Set aside shrimp.

In the frying pan, heat 3 tablespoons of the butter, then slowly blend in flour; cook until bubbly. Gradually stir in cooking liquid and cook, stirring, until thickened. Taste and add more salt if needed. Return shrimp to pan; cover and simmer about 3 minutes, or until shrimp are tender, but not overcooked.

Add remaining 2 tablespoons butter, quickly blend in cream, reheat, and remove from heat. Pour shrimp and sauce into serving dish, sprinkle with the grated cheese, and bring to the table for serving.

Makes 4 servings.

❦ Abalone Mexicana ❦

"In addition to legislating, I also enjoy a hobby of skin diving," says Bob Wilson. "I have served many delicious abalone steaks, freshly caught off the coastal rocks of Southern California."

The abalone is not a food that will stand much tampering; you can over-season it very easily. But tiny flecks of green pepper, and lime wedges on the side, pick it up just enough to make a worthwhile variation.

1 pound sliced, pounded abalone
2 eggs
½ cup tomato sauce
¾ cup medium-sized cracker crumbs
Paprika
¼ cup finely chopped green pepper
Butter
Salt
1 or more limes

Marinate abalone steaks in mixture of beaten eggs and tomato sauce for at least 30 minutes. Lift steaks from egg mixture and dip quickly in crumbs, coating each side. Sprinkle both sides of each steak with paprika and green pepper; pat lightly to hold pepper in place. Sauté in butter over medium high heat for not more than 1 minute on each side. Salt to taste. Garnish with wedges of lime. Makes 4 servings.

Poached Halibut with Shrimp

People so often eat fish fried—because the cook lacked other inspiration—that a recipe of a totally different nature affords pleasure indeed. J. Roger Kay carefully wraps halibut in cheesecloth, poaches it, and serves it with a subtly seasoned sauce.

If you like the fish more richly adorned, use more shrimp (either fresh or canned). But *do not overcook the halibut.*

2 pounds halibut (center slice, 1½ inches thick)
Water
2 teaspoons salt
6 whole allspice
1 bay leaf
6 whole black peppers
Juice of 1 lemon
¼ cup (½ cube) butter
¼ cup flour
⅛ teaspoon pepper
¼ teaspoon paprika
¾ cup liquid from cooking fish
¼ cup half-and-half (half cream, half milk)
Salt to taste
Lemon juice to taste
1 can (4½ oz.) shrimp, drained
Stuffed olives, halved

Rinse halibut in cold water. Wrap fish in cheesecloth, with enough extra cloth at each end to use for lifting. Place fish in shallow pan. Add water (to cover fish), salt, allspice, bay leaf, whole black peppers, and lemon juice. Cover and simmer gently 5 to 8 minutes—until fish will flake—but try to err in the direction of undercooking. Let it cool in the liquid.

In another pan, melt butter; stir in flour, pepper, paprika; and cook until bubbly. Gradually stir in ¾ cup of liquid in which fish was cooked and the half-and-half. Stir over low heat until mixture thickens. Add additional salt and lemon juice to taste. Finely chop shrimp, reserving a few whole ones for garnish, and add the chopped shrimp to the white sauce.

Carefully lift fish to heat-resistant serving platter. Remove cheesecloth. Spread sauce over fish as you would ice a cake. Garnish with whole shrimp and stuffed olives. Heat in moderate oven (350°) about 10 minutes, or until just barely heated through. Makes 4 to 6 servings.

❈ Spanish Rice with Shrimp ❈

Put onion and tomato and green pepper with rice, and you have Spanish Rice, give or take a few seasonings either way. But then add shrimp—thanks to S. E. Lovett—and you have an ideal rounding-out with something more solid than just the starch and vegetables, not to mention a more distinctive dish in general. The important thing is not to overcook the shrimp and make it tough.

2 tablespoons butter
3 tablespoons finely chopped onion
4 tablespoons chopped green pepper
2 cups shrimp, shelled and deveined
1½ cups cooked rice
1½ cups canned tomatoes (or tomato soup)
1 cup fresh mushrooms
½ teaspoon salt, or to taste
¼ teaspoon pepper

Melt butter, add onion and green pepper, and fry over moderate heat for 3 minutes. Add shrimp and cook 3 minutes. Add rice, tomatoes, mushrooms, salt, and pepper. Cook, stirring, for 2 or 3 minutes. Cover, let simmer 10 minutes. Makes 4 to 6 servings.

❈ Smoky Shrimp Skewer ❈

Robert J. Zanotti has a very quick shrimp barbecue method to propose. The instant-type prepared marinade provides salt and penetrates the shellfish just enough for some of the other flavorings to be absorbed slightly. But it's very important that you just dip the shrimp in the marinade for a moment, then remove and cook immediately. If you allow it to remain longer, the texture of the shrimp is apt to get too mushy, and it may get too salty. If you do it just right, it should be pleasantly smoky and mildly herbed with basil, tarragon, and celery seed. The little trick of butterflying the shrimp also makes it look more impressive than usual.

2 pounds large uncooked shrimp or prawns
(about 12 to 14 shrimp per lb.)
1 package instant meat marinade
⅓ cup dry white wine
⅓ cup lime or lemon juice
2 tablespoons salad oil
½ teaspoon basil
½ teaspoon tarragon
½ teaspoon celery seed

Shell and devein raw shrimp, leaving tails on. Split along the back curve, cutting almost to the inner edge; open and press flat. Mix packaged marinade, following package directions but using the wine and lemon juice in place of the water the directions call for. Add salad oil and seasonings and blend thoroughly.

Skewer the shrimp on four to six skewers. Dip skewered shrimp into the marinade, drain, and place immediately on grill about 4 inches above glowing coals. Cook until shrimp turn pink, about 2 to 3 minutes per side. Baste frequently. Serve immediately. Makes 4 to 6 servings.

Half-Time Scallops

"On a crisp, clear, fall day, watching a professional football game on television, I got the urge to create a light noonday snack involving scallops and with a really different herb and wine flavor," says Harlowe J. Longfelder.

He played his hunch exactly right, and his timing and coordination are excellent. "This dish doesn't take much preparation (if your wife has remembered to remove the scallops from the freezer), and the cooking can be accomplished during the half-time of the game." What could be neater?

1 pound scallops
3 tablespoons olive oil
1 clove garlic, crushed
1 tablespoon tarragon vinegar
⅛ teaspoon oregano
⅛ teaspoon basil
½ cup sauterne
Salt and pepper to taste
Finely chopped parsley

Defrost, wash, dry scallops. Heat olive oil in large skillet over high heat; add scallops with garlic and sauté for about 3 minutes, turning frequently. Remove pan from heat; reduce heat to medium low. Add vinegar, oregano, basil, sauterne, salt and pepper. Place pan on heat and simmer for 5 minutes, stirring occasionally. (Do not overcook.)

Meanwhile, toast and butter some small and fairly thin slices of sourdough French bread. Serve scallops and juice in flat soup bowls, sprinkled with chopped parsley. Use the bread to enjoy the flavorful juice. Suggest serving sliced tomatoes and a glass of the wine with the scallops.

Makes 2 to 4 servings.

Oysters a la Osage

In the Oklahoma hills Frank R. Brown learned this recipe. And a very unlikely place it was to have learned it. He explains in the following anecdote:

"Mother was born in Kansas in 1879. Her family moved to Hot Springs, Arkansas, where in her twentieth year she met and married my father, who was one-quarter Osage Indian from the Indian Territory, now Oklahoma. I was born on his ranch there, and eating this oyster dish on cold winter evenings is one of my favorite early memories."

Where Mrs. Brown obtained her oysters is a puzzle, but she did it "someplace, somehow, somewhere," for which we are as thankful as her son. Chef Brown reminisces, "The cream was from our spring house, the butter was homemade, the crackers from a cracker barrel, and the nutmeg hand-grated from the nut as needed."

1 pint oysters (cut if large)
⅛ teaspoon freshly grated nutmeg
⅛ teaspoon salt
¼ teaspoon pepper
6 slices bacon, cooked crisp and crumbled
1 cup shredded Swiss cheese
1 cup heavy cream
½ cup coarsely broken crackers
2 tablespoons butter

Grease a shallow 1½-quart baking dish. Arrange the oysters and their juices in the dish, grate nutmeg over them, and sprinkle on salt and pepper. Sprinkle on the bacon and cheese, pour the cream over all, then cover with cracker crumbs and dot with butter. Bake uncovered in a hot oven (400°) for 20 minutes. Makes about 4 servings.

A cheer for Oklahoma and oysters.

⚜ Crab Concorde ⚜

Here's a dish to be done in the French manner with whatever *savoir faire* and aplomb you can manage at the moment. It will probably be enough, because the dish is pretty nearly idiot-proof.

"The only drawback to serving a 'Concorde' often," says Mike Costa of his recipe, "is that calorie counting must be dismissed as inconsequential. After all, one can always diet tomorrow. Bon appetit."

> 2 cups cooked crab
> About ⅔ cup butter
> Pinch of salt
> ½ teaspoon pepper
> ½ cup cream, or half-and-half
> ½ cup shredded Cheddar cheese
> ½ teaspoon curry powder
> ½ cup sliced mushrooms
> 1½ teaspoons finely chopped onion
> 1½ teaspoons minced garlic
> ½ cup soft bread crumbs
> 1 large tomato, sliced
> 6 medium-sized mushroom caps
> 6 stuffed large green olives
> 1 ounce brandy or cognac

Heat the crab thoroughly in 3 tablespoons of the butter, melted. Stir slightly. Do not brown. Add salt and pepper. Reserve.

In a saucepan, heat the cream to just below boiling, then reduce heat and add cheese. Stir until cheese is melted and sauce is very smooth. Add curry and continue stirring. When all is thoroughly mixed and smooth, add the crab. Stir.

Sauté sliced mushrooms, onions, and garlic in 1 tablespoon of the butter just long enough to evaporate the liquid that the mushrooms will throw off and to soften the onions and garlic. Then add crab sauce mixture. Turn into 1½-quart baking dish.

Prepare a *chapelure* by thoroughly mixing bread crumbs with about 2 tablespoons of the butter. Spread this preparation evenly over the crab and dot the surface with bits of butter. Place under broiler just long enough to melt the surface butter and brown the chapelure lightly.

While the chapelure is browning, sauté the sliced tomato and mushroom caps separately in 2 tablespoons butter each. The sliced tomatoes should be watched carefully during this process so they will not lose their shape.

Remove crab from broiler. Carefully place tomato slices in a line across the center of the crab mixture, overlapping the slices. Place mushroom caps, tops up, around the edge of the baking dish, and center a slice of stuffed green olive on top of each cap.

Heat brandy, pour over the dish, light it, and present flaming. Makes 6 servings as a first course.

A chilled dry wine is a perfect accompaniment.

⚞ Oysters Labrador ⚟

For a nippy evening at home or in a snow country cabin, Charles Bock's oysters are strongly recommended. They could also be relished in considerably warmer weather; however, the warming effect of this stew-like soup—or vice versa—pleases the inner man most when the outer man is a bit chilly.

In place of hot biscuits or toast, you might substitute crackers, pilot biscuit, or croutons in the manner of French onion soup.

¼ cup diced carrots
¼ cup diced onions
2 tablespoons diced celery
4 tablespoons butter
3 tablespoons flour
1 can (8 oz.) oysters, with their juice
1½ cups milk
¼ teaspoon salt
⅛ teaspoon pepper
⅛ teaspoon dry mustard
½ teaspoon Worcestershire
1 tablespoon parsley
Hot biscuits (about 2 cups biscuit mix
should be ample) or toast

Lightly sauté the carrots, onions, and celery in the butter; stir in the flour and continue cooking until bubbly. Gradually stir in the juice of the oysters and milk, and cook until thickened. Add all seasonings and also the oysters. When the oysters are heated, serve over hot biscuits or toast. Makes 4 to 6 servings.

⚞ Dungeness Crab Fritters ⚟

Jack M. Saad has a special interest in seafood of all kinds. He will tell you that one of the joys of living along much of the West Coast during the cold months is fresh Dungeness crab. Where it's not available fresh, the frozen variety will do for his fritters, and once it's out of season you can even try canned.

½ pound fresh or frozen Dungeness crab meat
or 1 can (about 8 oz.) crab meat
2 tablespoons chopped green onion
1 tablespoon chopped parsley
1 tablespoon chopped green pepper
2 tablespoons chopped ripe tomato
2 eggs, slightly beaten
1 teaspoon Worcestershire
¼ cup unsifted flour
2 teaspoons baking powder
⅛ teaspoon salt
3 tablespoons butter or shortening
Lemon wedges (optional)
Tartar sauce (optional)

Thoroughly mix together the crab, onion, parsley, green pepper, tomato, eggs, and Worcestershire. Sift together into the crab mixture the flour, baking powder, and salt. Stir just until blended. Heat the butter or shortening in a frying pan over moderately high heat. Fry tablespoonfuls of the crab mixture, turning once to brown well on both sides. Serve with lemon wedges or tartar sauce. Makes about 16 fritters.

EGGS, RICE, PASTA

Here are foods that offer great opportunities to men who like to improvise and invent new dishes. The recipes in this chapter are proof indeed that there are ways with an egg other than frying, ways with pasta other than just boiling.

The dishes tend to defy classification, but they include some unusual concoctions, as well as names: Eggs and Onions, Mushroom Velvet, Stuffed Chiles Marinara, and Four-Cheese Lasagna, for example. Some of the chefs have drawn their inspiration from French, Italian, Chinese, or Mexican cuisines (you'll encounter green chiles several times as a surprise ingredient).

Quite a number of the recipes seem to be earmarked for Sunday morning; "that is my time to wrap the dish towel around my middle and let my taste imagination run unhindered," one man confesses.

Throughout you will notice that eggs in any form and the various kinds of cheese, rice, and pasta, take kindly to additions and seasonings by a cook who is not too inhibited.

⚜ Roman Cheese Pie ⚜

Consider the egg. During the Christmas season of good will, you encounter it usually in such friendly concoctions as eggnog and Tom-and-Jerry, but it serves equally well at binding up a stuffing mixture or puffing up a soufflé (to mention only two of multiple possibilities).

Handy for holiday entertaining, Kenneth Stearns calls this contribution a Roman Cheese Pie, but it might be aptly called a *quizza*, since it is a kind of basic quiche with pizza flavors. You could serve it as an appetizer, a dinner first course, the main course of a light lunch, or a late-at-night snack.

1 cup shredded Cheddar cheese
2 eggs, slightly beaten
1 teaspoon minced onion
½ teaspoon dry mustard
½ teaspoon salt
Freshly ground pepper to taste
8-inch unbaked pastry shell
½ medium-sized tomato, peeled and thinly sliced
¼ green pepper, cut in thin strips
1 pre-cooked Italian sausage, sliced
Dash oregano
Salt to taste
Pepper to taste

Combine the cheese, eggs, onion, mustard, salt, and pepper; pour into the pastry shell. Arrange tomato slices, green pepper strips, and sausage over the surface, and sprinkle with the oregano, salt, and pepper. Bake in a moderate oven (350°) for 30 minutes, or until firmly set. Makes 4 servings as a main course.

⚜ Sunday Breakfast Special ⚜

Earl Chalk concerns himself with Sunday breakfast. What he offers to pour over the poached eggs is definitely worth the pouring. The result may remind you of Eggs Benedict, although it's quite different and takes far less attention to timing than that classic and complex dish. With perfect eggs on crusty buttered English muffins, this is delicious.

2 tablespoons butter or margarine
2 tablespoons finely chopped fresh mushrooms
⅛ teaspoon salt
Dash pepper
½ cup commercial sour cream
⅛ teaspoon Worcestershire
¼ teaspoon dry mustard
¼ cup shredded sharp Cheddar cheese
6 poached eggs
3 English muffins, split, toasted, and buttered

Melt butter in saucepan, add chopped mushrooms, and brown lightly. Stir in salt, pepper, sour cream, Worcestershire, mustard, and cheese, and stir over low heat until cheese melts. Prepare 6 poached eggs and place them on muffin halves. Pour over warm sauce and serve immediately. Makes 6 servings.

※ Eggs Restauratifs ※

Festive evenings are very popular these days, and A. Hart, Jr., proposes a specific for the mornings that follow.

"On those certain mornings when the palate requires something a little more piquant than usual, by accidental inspiration I developed what has now become a standard prescription either served at the conclusion of festivities or as a brunch the following morning with the whole family joining in and/or any leftover guests." Multiply the ingredients by the number of people you are serving.

1 slice bacon
1 slice bread
Butter
1 large slice tomato
1 egg
1 tablespoon water
Slice (about 2 oz.) Cheddar cheese
½ tablespoon Worcestershire
Salt to taste
Pepper to taste
Paprika to taste

Fry bacon until almost crisp. Meanwhile, trim crusts from bread, place under broiler, and toast on one side only; butter the untoasted side. Remove bacon from pan, drain off excess drippings, and gently fry tomato in same pan; then remove and place on buttered toast. Place egg in same pan, add water, cover, and cook until yolk is just firm enough so it won't run. Place on tomato. Cut cheese into very small pieces and place on egg. Sprinkle with Worcestershire, salt, pepper, and paprika. Cut bacon slice in half and place on top of cheese.

Slip the whole assembly under the broiler until the cheese has melted. Place on a hot plate and serve immediately. Makes 1 serving.

※ Conchiglie Pescatore ※

In the realm of delicate *pasta* dishes, it's hard to beat Italian cookery, particularly that of northern Italy where the tomato isn't laid on too heavily. Thomas M. Conrow has created a dish which follows that great tradition.

1 package (12 oz.) seashell macaroni (*Conchiglia*)
Salt to taste
Water
¾ cup (⅜ lb.) margarine or butter
1½ teaspoons dried basil
3 teaspoons dried parsley
1 can (about 6 oz.) tiny Pacific shrimp or chopped clams
1 teaspoon sherry
Grated Parmesan cheese

Cook macaroni in salted water. Meanwhile prepare sauce: Put margarine or butter in saucepan and melt gently over low heat. Add basil and parsley; heat. Add shrimp or clams; you can add a bit of the canned shrimp or clam juice for flavor. Add sherry.

When macaroni is cooked *al dente*, drain well and place in serving dish. Add sauce and sprinkle with Parmesan cheese to taste. Toss well and serve. Makes 6 to 8 servings.

🦅 Imaginative Eggs 🦅

"Sunday morning is my time to wrap the dish towel around my middle and let my taste imagination run unhindered," confesses James G. Oyler. "I'll admit some of my experiments were quickly forgotten and the local pancake house filled the void; however, this breakfast dish has weathered several months."

It is impressive how skillfully the many ingredients are blended in this recipe. The individual flavors come through clearly, but they don't clash.

4 slices bacon, chopped
2 slices boiled ham, slivered
1 tomato, peeled and sliced
2 canned green chiles, cut into strips
5 eggs
¼ teaspoon salt
Dash of pepper
Several dashes liquid hot-pepper seasoning
4 to 6 thin slices jack cheese
1 ripe avocado

Fry the chopped bacon until almost crisp. Add ham, tomato, and green chiles; cover pan and allow to simmer, stirring occasionally. When most of the liquid has boiled away, add the eggs beaten with the salt, pepper, and liquid hot-pepper seasoning. Again cover and allow eggs to set. Stir carefully now and then in order to cook the eggs uniformly. When eggs are set, place slices of cheese on top, cover again, and let the cheese melt. Serve immediately with thin slices of avocado on top. Makes 2 generous servings.

You may substitute sausage for other meat, or use bacon only. Mushrooms may also be added.

🦅 And Eggs and Onions 🦅

Nicholas Roosevelt once dedicated a cookbook to his "fellow members of the American Garlic Society." Here's a recipe for their blood brothers in the Onion Society.

Ken Kolsbun explains how-it-all-began: "Three of us fellows batched together while attending Cal Poly at Pomona. Here's a favorite of ours when the budget got low; it's easy to prepare, and good for breakfast, lunch, or dinner."

Oh lovers of the onion, it *is* good! And how simple. Serve it hot, perhaps with steak, or as a side dish at a buffet. For a main dish, some might want to increase the proportion of egg.

1 to 2 medium-sized yellow onions per person
Salt to taste
Shortening
1 to 2 eggs per person

Slice, salt, and fry onions in shortening until light brown and tender. Just before removing from heat, pour over beaten eggs. Stir the mixture. The eggs will cling to the onions and vice versa. The dish is filling, like meat. Serve immediately.

ᔡ Four-Cheese Lasagna ᔡ

Not all good things come in small packages. Henry George Watkins' cheese lasagna serves, without inordinate stretching, a tableful of people.

You need four kinds of cheese, three of them Italian, to make this dish, so if you have an Italian delicatessen or cheese shop at hand, proceed there at once. If you don't, all the cheeses are available in the dairy food section of large markets.

2 tablespoons olive oil
¾ pound ground beef chuck
¼ cup minced onion
1½ teaspoons garlic powder
1½ teaspoons monosodium glutamate
2 cans (7½ oz. each) mushroom sauce
1 can (3 or 4 oz.) sliced mushrooms
1 can (about 3½ oz.) pitted black olives, drained and chopped
½ bay leaf
2 tablespoons dry red wine or water
½ teaspoon salt
⅛ teaspoon pepper
6 ounces lasagna
Boiling, salted water
½ pound ricotta cheese
1¼ cups grated Parmesan or Romano cheese
½ pound mozzarella, shredded
½ pound mild Cheddar cheese, shredded

For the meat sauce, heat oil in a heavy frying pan over medium heat, crumble meat into the pan, and add onion and garlic powder and monosodium glutamate. Cook, stirring, until meat loses pink color. Add mushroom sauce, mushrooms (including liquid), olives, bay leaf, wine, salt, and pepper and simmer ½ hour, or until somewhat thickened. Remove bay leaf.

While the meat is cooking, cook the lasagna in boiling, salted water until just tender. Drain. In a large casserole (9 by 13 by 2 inches) arrange a layer of cooked lasagna, a layer of meat sauce, and a layer of each of the cheeses using about a third of each. Continue, layering ingredients, finishing with cheese on top. Bake, uncovered, in a moderate oven (375°) about 40 minutes, or until heated through and bubbly. Makes 6 to 8 servings.

❧ Ojos de Buey (Ox Eyes) ❧

"California-Sonora cookery used to have some twists different from other sections of Mexico," says Ted Hutchinson. "Among these was the preparation and seasoning of the red chile sauce—and ostracism to the heretic who doped it up with contaminating tomato. The red chile sauce here is like that prepared by the early Californians."

The amount of red chile sauce has been tempered to pamper tender-mouthed eaters. But if you'd like it hotter than the hinges, just pour on the chile sauce to replace any or all of the consommé. This happens to be an egg dish, by the way.

> 1 tablespoon flour
> 1 tablespoon bacon drippings
> ½ can (10 oz.) enchilada sauce (made with red chiles)
> ½ can (10 oz.) consommé
> 4 eggs
> Salt to taste
> Pepper to taste
> Jack cheese or Cheddar (optional)

In a skillet, brown flour in drippings and then add enchilada sauce and consommé. Simmer until slightly thickened. Add eggs and poach as desired. Season lightly with salt and pepper (sauce is already seasoned). Strip with cheese or sprinkle with grated cheese, if desired. Spoon sauce over the eggs before serving, and accompany with warm tortillas. Makes 2 tasty servings.

❧ Tyrol Tarts ❧

"The recipe that follows is simply an individual Swiss cheese pie—though an extraordinarily flavored one," says Fred Cherry. "I'd call it that—if I weren't captivated by the alliterative lilt of 'Tyrol Tarts.'"

A private poll was taken of those who'd tasted this on when to serve these tarts, the enthusiastic responses covered morning, noon, and night.

> 3 slices bacon
> 3 tablespoons finely chopped onion
> 4 eggs
> ¼ cup milk
> ¼ cup commercial sour cream
> 1 teaspoon caraway seed
> ¼ teaspoon freshly ground pepper
> ⅔ teaspoon salt
> 1½ cups shredded Swiss cheese
> 6 small unbaked pie shells (about 4 inches)
> Additional pepper and caraway seed

Fry bacon until very crisp, drain well, and chop it coarsely. Sauté onion in 1 tablespoon of the bacon fat. Beat eggs thoroughly and stir in the milk, sour cream, caraway seed, pepper, salt, Swiss cheese, and bacon. Pour mixture into small pie shells and sprinkle with pepper and caraway seed. Bake in a moderate oven (350°) for 20 minutes, or until a knife inserted comes out clean. Serve hot or cold. Makes 6 servings.

Ham and Eggs Cantonese

Any sliced cold cuts or canned luncheon meat could go into Jim Blanchfield's slightly Chinese version of scrambled eggs, but the kind of meat recommended most highly is one of the mildest in flavor: boiled ham.

In this recipe the Chinese oyster sauce is the only seasoning. It also eliminates any need for salt.

4 eggs
¼ cup milk
½ cup diced ham
1 green onion, diced
1 tablespoon Chinese oyster sauce
1 teaspoon wheat germ (optional)
Butter

Mix all ingredients thoroughly and scramble in a buttered pan. Makes 2 servings.

Mushroom Velvet

There is no rule that the name of a recipe should reveal its contents. That wouldn't seem fair in this era when you don't expect the same from a novel, play, or movie title. "Velvet" in the title of Sam Swisher's recipe covers a multitude of delicacies, and it could be that mushroom is merely one of the incidentals.

With the greens and the eggs and the flavorings, it has a pleasing play of textures. The soy sauce and the stir-fry cooking relate it to Chinese and Japanese cookery. It's a braw dish for a brunch.

1 pound fresh mushrooms
4 tablespoons salad oil
1 small leek, quartered and sliced thin
2 green onions and their tops, minced
2 tablespoons parsley, minced
3 tablespoons soy sauce
½ teaspoon monosodium glutamate
1 dozen fresh eggs
Dash cayenne
1 cup fresh watercress leaves

Wash mushrooms and drain (half-dollar size is ideal; otherwise, cut into bite-sized pieces). Slice the stems into thin pieces. Place oil in large skillet until hot. Add leek and sauté 1 minute over high heat. Add green onions and sauté 1 minute. Add parsley and sauté 1 minute. Add mushroom tops and stems and sauté 3 minutes. (Keep stirring constantly through all the foregoing additions.)

Mix soy sauce and monosodium glutamate and pour over mushrooms. Stir and cover for 2 minutes.

Break eggs into a dish but leave whole; do not beat. Uncover mushrooms and pour eggs over. Do not stir until whites have partially set up. Then stir gently but thoroughly adding cayenne, and then watercress. Cook just until the yolks set up. Remove from heat immediately so eggs will be tender and watercress crisp. Serve immediately. Makes 6 servings.

Serve it for brunch with fresh garden grapefruit, wholewheat biscuits, mountain honey, and plenty of hot coffee.

❧ Chiles Rellenos Digresion ❧

The classic Mexican recipe for *Chiles Rellenos* calls for wrapping chiles around the cheese, dropping each in an egg-and-flour batter, and cooking very carefully.

The classic recipe justly deserves its fame; but don't look down your nose at the variation which Charles A. Owen has developed. "Chiles Rellenos have been a favorite in our family. But with the usual recipes, the cook is cooking while everyone eats. Other means were needed so the cook could mingle with the guests." The egg mixture fluffs up a little like a soufflé in this recipe, and the cheese is more evident throughout than in the traditional dish.

6 eggs
1 tablespoon flour
¼ teaspoon salt
¼ teaspoon pepper, or to taste
1 can (4 oz.) green chiles
½ pound mild Cheddar or jack cheese

Separate eggs. Beat egg whites until stiff. Mix flour, salt, and pepper with egg yolks; then fold in beaten egg whites and pour half of this mixture into a greased 2 by 7 by 13-inch baking dish.

Wash chiles and remove seeds. Spread chiles over egg batter and then cover with cheese slices. Pour rest of egg mixture over cheese. Bake 25 minutes in a 325° oven. Cut in 3-inch squares and serve with a Mexican hot sauce if desired. Delicious with tortillas, refried beans, and cole slaw. Makes 4 servings.

❧ Creamed Rice with a Bite ❧

It's well to be properly prepared before you first try the Creamed Rice proposed by William Talbot Bergeson. It's an intriguing mixture of green and white, sharpness and blandness—like a starch dish and a salad combined in one. As such, it makes a remarkably good complement for almost any meat. The green chiles give it just the right amount of "bite."

"It's hot to the taste," says one partaker, "but it grows on you. Take a bite—eat something else—then you're drawn back to the rice again and again. It's crazy, because I don't like 'hot' food."

3 cups water
1 cup long grain rice
½ cup (1 cube) butter or margarine
1 cup drained, chopped canned green chiles
1 cup commercial sour cream, mixed with 3 heaping tablespoons chopped chives an hour before cooking
½ teaspoon salt
¼ teaspoon white pepper

Bring water to a boil; add rice, reduce heat, tightly cover the pan and steam until tender. Add butter, replace cover, and allow butter to melt. Add remaining ingredients, stir gently until completely mixed, serve immediately. Makes 4 to 6 servings.

⋙ Spaghetti Sauce Sicilienne ⋙

An Italian-style meat sauce has to meet certain standards before it is good enough to slather over a platter of spaghetti or other pasta cooked to just the right degree of tenderness. All the good sauces are such blends of many foods and seasonings that it is often difficult to detect striking differences.

John V. Hughes has made up the recipe for this sauce with a knowledge born of long food experience—including 32 years as a professional chef and a lifetime of adding recipes to his private collection, which he now estimates at 12,000 to 15,000.

Perhaps the most distinctive feature of this sauce is its inclusion of both green and ripe olives. But first taste it and make your own comparisons.

½ cup finely chopped onion
2 tablespoons olive oil
1 pound lean ground beef (or equal parts beef, veal, and pork)
3 cloves garlic, finely minced or mashed
¼ cup finely chopped green pepper
2 cans (1 lb. each) tomatoes, crushed
2 cans (8 oz. each) tomato sauce
1 can (3 oz.) sliced broiled mushrooms
¼ cup finely chopped parsley
1½ teaspoons oregano
½ teaspoon ground cumin
Salt to taste
½ teaspoon black pepper, or to taste
½ teaspoon monosodium glutamate
¼ teaspoon ground thyme
1 bay leaf
1 cup water or dry red wine
¼ cup sliced and pitted ripe olives
¼ cup sliced stuffed green olives
1 tablespoon dark brown sugar
1 teaspoon lemon juice
2 tablespoons grated Parmesan cheese

Cook onions in hot olive oil until golden. Add meat and garlic and brown slightly. Drain fat from meat mixture and discard. Add all remaining ingredients; simmer uncovered for 2 to 2½ hours or longer (it takes long, slow cooking to make a really good sauce), until sauce is nice and thick. Stir occasionally. Remove bay leaf. Makes enough sauce for about 1½ pounds spaghetti, cooked.

⋙ Enchiladas de Arroz y Queso ⋘

Dick Thompson's enchiladas might never have reached us if his family hadn't insisted, "Dad, please write *this one* down!" Dick says: "These enchiladas were the happy result of our having leftover rice in the refrigerator. My wife is some kind of nut about using up leftovers in a tasty manner, so I decided to get into the act. We all love spicy Mexican food, and this went over very well."

As is, this dish is decidedly peppery. It should normally be served with a meat dish of some kind for a full meal; but it can stand alone with just a good green salad for a light lunch.

1 can (10 oz.) red chile sauce
¾ pound Longhorn or mild Cheddar cheese
6 tablespoons butter or margarine
1 large onion, finely chopped
3 stalks celery, thinly sliced
1 can (about 4 oz.) chopped black olives, drained
1 can (4 oz.) California green chiles,
     seeded, and chopped
3 cups cooked white rice
3 tablespoons salad oil
1 dozen corn tortillas

Heat chile sauce to boiling and set aside. Shred cheese and set aside. Melt butter in frying pan, add onions and celery, and cook over low heat until onion is transparent (about 10 minutes). Remove about a fourth of this mixture, mix with chopped olives, and set aside.

To remaining onion-celery mixture, add chopped chiles and cooked rice. Add about ⅓ of red chile sauce and cook over low heat for 2 to 3 minutes. Remove from heat and set aside. In a small frying pan, heat salad oil over high heat, then fry each tortilla on each side quickly. (They should be soft.)

To assemble enchiladas, spread about 1 tablespoonful red chile sauce over each tortilla. Divide rice mixture among the 12 tortillas, then spread about 2 teaspoons olive mixture and 1 tablespoon shredded cheese down the center of each. Roll around filling and place seam-side-down in a buttered 9 by 13-inch baking dish. Once tortillas are filled, pour any remaining red chile sauce and sprinkle any remaining cheese over top. Bake in a moderately hot oven (375°) for 15 minutes or until enchiladas are heated throughout. Serve with a meat entrée and green salad. Makes about 12 enchiladas.

⚓ Winebibber's Feathered Rice ⚓

Any dish with a name like Winebibber's Feathered Rice should win a few followers. The amount of winebibbing involved here is rather slight. Actually the rice imbibes the wine, which makes up half the liquid that is eventually absorbed into rice during the cooking process. Dennis Ojakangas adds salt, butter, mushrooms, and onions, but no other seasoning—thus it forms a reasonable, neutral background for a meat dish that might well be seasoned more exotically. The term feathered rice means simply fluffy rice.

1 cup rice
½ cup sliced mushrooms
1 small onion, diced
¼ cup (½ cube) butter
1 cup wine (pick your favorite)
1½ cups water
1 teaspoon salt

Place rice—unwashed—in a shallow pan and roast uncovered in a moderate (350°) oven until it is golden brown. Meanwhile sauté mushrooms and onions in butter. When the rice has roasted to a golden brown, place it in a 2-quart casserole with a cover.

Combine the wine, water, and salt in a saucepan and bring to a boil; add along with sautéed mushrooms and onions to the rice. Stir. Cover and place in a moderate oven (350°) for 30 minutes. Don't peek, or the rice will not fluff. Makes 4 servings.

⚓ Three-Lingo Rice ⚓

Colonel Benjamin C. Allin, III, presented his dish in three languages: *Risotto con Vongoli, Arroz con Almejas*, and the one most of us know best, Rice with Clams.
The flavors are subtle, well blended, but easily overpowered by other more rough and ready characters if you should do a careless job of planning the menu.

¼ cube (2 tablespoons) butter or margarine
1 onion, minced
¼ teaspoon oregano
¼ teaspoon dried celery leaves
¼ teaspoon monosodium glutamate
¼ teaspoon salt
⅛ teaspoon black pepper
⅛ teaspoon cayenne
1 cup rice
2 tablespoons brandy (optional)
⅓ cup dry white wine
1 bottle (8 oz.) clam nectar
Liquid from a can of minced clams
Water
3 tablespoons grated Parmesan cheese
1 can (about 7 oz.) minced clams

Melt butter or margarine on top of range in a casserole dish (one which can be used over direct heat). Add onion and cook until browned. Add all seasonings and rice, and cook, stirring with wooden spoon. When rice has turned shiny white, slowly add brandy and wine, stirring until liquid is cooked out. Then combine clam nectar, liquid from canned clams, and enough water to make a total of 2¼ cups liquid. Add to previous mixture in casserole; bring to a boil. Cover and bake in moderate oven (350°) for 30 minutes, or until rice is tender.

Remove from oven and stir in cheese and clams. Return to oven, uncovered, and bake for 10 minutes. Serve. Makes 4 or 5 servings.

VERSATILE VEGETABLES

It is still fashionable to say mean things about vegetables, especially among men who grew up learning to hate them because of age-old methods of preparing them. Among the meanest ever said about vegetables are these words by a poet named Roy Campbell:

"Far in the desert we have been
Where Nature, still to poets kind,
Admits no vegetable green
To soften the determined mind."

Fortunately, there have been some new developments admitted in vegetable cookery. And they have not escaped the attention of alert male cooks.

Don't search this chapter for recipes using peas, carrots, string beans, or beets. These vegetables evidently present no particular problems or challenges to adventurous men cooks. They prefer to give their attention to the round kind of beans—which men like far better than do most women—and to the hitherto unrealized potentialities of such vegetables as mushrooms, green tomatoes, cabbage, pimientos, eggplant, asparagus, zucchini, turnips, and Brussels sprouts.

⚜ Idaho Potato Bake ⚜

If the other people in Idaho serve baked potatoes the way Claude H. Northway does, they don't need much else for their dinners. These are plenty hearty. Try them for a heavy meal after you've been out all day hunting bear, or tending your trap lines, or just tramping in the woods. Or just serve them any time you darn well please.

4 medium to large potatoes
8 slices bacon
1 cup milk
1 tablespoon grated green pepper
1 teaspoon grated onion
1 tablespoon finely diced celery
2 tablespoons melted butter or bacon drippings
Salt to taste
Pepper to taste
Milk

Bake the potatoes. Shortly before they are done, fry bacon until crisp and set aside, saving drippings.

Remove potatoes from oven, cut in two, and scoop out centers as close to skin as possible without breaking; mash the potato pulp. Heat milk to the boiling point; add green pepper, onion, celery, bacon drippings, salt and pepper; cook 3 minutes. Add this mixture to the mashed potato and beat until light and fluffy. Crumble 6 slices of cooked bacon into small bits and fold into potato mixture. Fill potato shells with this mixture, brush with milk, crumble remaining bacon and sprinkle on top; return to oven to brown. Serve with fried trout or a big juicy steak and a green salad. Makes 4 servings.

⚜ Zucchini-Sherry Surprise ⚜

The big surprise in Dick Zediker's recipe is the celery. It and the onion tend to bracket the zucchini in both flavor and texture and give it a nice "frame of reference." Be sparing with liquid, and cook only until the zucchini is tender-crisp.

4 tablespoons butter
1½ cups chopped onion
1½ cups sliced celery
5 small zucchini, sliced
¼ cup rich chicken broth
¼ cup sherry
Salt to taste

Melt butter in a frying pan over high heat, then add onion and celery and stir constantly until the butter is gone. Turn down heat to medium, add zucchini and chicken broth, cover, and cook 5 minutes, or until zucchini is done to your liking, lifting lid and stirring occasionally. Just before serving, add sherry and salt if needed. Makes 6 servings.

⠶ Dearest Bill Beans ⠶

In former days and colder climates, the root cellar and preserve closet were stocked with the winter's supplies. By the time March arrived, apples were withering, potatoes sprouting, and everyone was ready for a powerful spring tonic.

These days the corner supermarket has edged out the root cellar, and a chef in need can always turn up a tomato, an orange, or an artichoke. (Root cellars are called cold storage now, and the apples are still there, but unwrinkled.)

From this happy vantage point, it's nice to look back to the old days, and the hearty, hot, winter meals in front of the roaring fire. W. J. Vorwerk suggests beans as a starter. He says of these beans, "The recipe grew out of a series of tries and tastes with one developed by a friend. The name was given by an affectionate member of the family of the originator. He approved the modifications."

So down to the root cellar for your side of bacon, your sack of onions, and a jar of molasses, and prepare to make Dearest Bill Beans.

6 slices bacon, chopped
1 large onion, chopped
3 cans (about 1 lb. each) kidney beans, drained
2 cans (8 oz. each) tomato sauce
1 tablespoon Worcestershire
1 tablespoon soy sauce
¼ teaspoon freshly ground pepper
¼ cup molasses
2 tablespoons red wine vinegar
1 chorizo (Mexican sausage), cut in ½-inch slices

Sauté bacon in a Dutch oven until partially cooked. Drain off all but about 2 tablespoons of the drippings. Add onions to the pan and continue cooking until they are transparent. Mash half of the drained beans, and add mashed and whole beans and all the remaining ingredients to bacon and onions. Stir, cover, and bake in a moderate oven (350°) for 30 minutes, or until heated through. Makes 6 to 8 servings.

⠶ Celery of the Islands ⠶

Good vegetable side dishes are always in demand. This one has "no calories (to speak of), not much food value, but taste and chew upon it and you'll forgive its other lacks," says Ed Mather. In essence, it is celery sautéed in butter and seasoned mainly with soy sauce.

4 cups sliced celery
2 tablespoons butter
2 tablespoons soy sauce
½ teaspoon sugar
¼ teaspoon freshly ground pepper

Use only the heavy outside stalks of the celery, without the foliage, and slice diagonally into 1-inch widths. Sauté celery in skillet in very hot butter until slightly browned, but still crisp when tested with a fork (4 to 8 minutes). Add remaining ingredients and stir 2 minutes longer, serve hot. Makes 4 servings.

ᐳᐳᐳ Three-Bean Cassoulet ᐊᐊᐊ

A dish that can wait gets extra points from every chef who likes to entertain unhurriedly. Such is this one from S. E. Vaughan.

"It is a variation of the classic Cassoulet, and was evolved because—by the time I got inspired to make it—I was forced to use ingenuity to circumvent the necessity of soaking any and all beans overnight."

So he used canned beans—three kinds. Also three meats and two wines. Almost everything is in multiples. It's a handsome dish to gaze upon and a husky one to eat. Men especially favor it.

> 1 can (1 lb.) red kidney beans
> 1 can (1 lb.) garbanzo beans
> 1 can (1 lb.) black-eyed peas
> ¼ teaspoon thyme
> ¼ teaspoon coarse-ground black pepper
> 1 bay leaf
> 2 large onions
> ¼ pound lean pork
> ¼ pound lean veal
> 4 tablespoons olive oil
> 1 cup white wine
> ½ cup muscatel
> 6 little pork sausages

Open cans of beans and pour contents into large bowl with thyme, pepper, and bay leaf crumbled fine. Mix well. Quarter onions and place in a 2-quart casserole. Pour bean mixture on top. Cover and bake 2 hours in a 225° oven.

Meanwhile cut pork and veal into small pieces and brown in olive oil. Pour over wine mixture and simmer, covered, until beans are ready.

Fry sausage and discard the grease. Cut sausages into small pieces and add to meat. Stir combined meat and sausage into bean casserole and pour over wine mixture in which meat has simmered. Add water if necessary so liquid just shows in the casserole. Cover and return to oven to bake for an additional two hours or so.

Makes 6 hearty servings.

⚞ Smoky Bean Simmer ⚟

Returning again and again to the lowly bean is a pretty general masculine tendency. And many who share it aren't really satisfied when you give them easy ways to cook beans. There are those hardy ones who prefer the long-drawn-out cooking process that seems more like a tribal ritual. If you can't soak the beans all night and then cook them all day, just what is this newfangled darn-fool world coming to?

Now Carl O. Schulte goes along willingly with the ritual. But he breaks step in two significant ways: He adds not one, but three kinds of meat, in generous quantity considering that beans are pretty heavy in protein, too. He also barbecues the beef and the sausage to give the whole dish smokiness, or, as he calls it, a unique "outdoorish" taste. "As interesting a bean as I've ever eaten," was one tasters apt summing-up.

"Normally I double this recipe to serve about 65 or more," says Carl, "but for this purpose I have cut amounts in half. These beans may be frozen and kept in a freezer for use at a future date without loss of flavor."

3 pounds (8 cups) small pink beans
Water
6 quarts meat stock or canned beef bouillon
1 medium-sized ham bone
1 pound bacon, sliced
8 cloves garlic, minced or mashed
¾ cup onion, finely chopped
3 cups mushrooms, diced
3 pounds lean chuck, ground (or ground round)
1 package (1 lb.) link sausages
6 cups solid pack canned tomatoes, broken up
2 cans (6 oz.) tomato paste
2 cans (8 oz.) Spanish-style tomato sauce
1½ teaspoons oregano
6 teaspoons salt, or to taste
3 teaspoons monosodium glutamate
2 teaspoons ground cumin seed
2 tablespoons chile con carne seasoning
3 tablespoons flour

Wash and pick over beans, put in electric roaster or large kettle, cover with water, and soak overnight. Next morning, pour off water; add meat stock or bouillon and the ham bone. Add more water, if necessary, so beans are fully covered. Cook, covered, about 2 hours. Then remove ham bone and prepare the other ingredients as follows:

Dice bacon, fry until crisp, and add to beans. Fry garlic, onion, and mushrooms in bacon fat until onion becomes golden brown; then add all to beans. Form ground meat into large thick patties or squares and slowly barbecue over charcoal until done; also barbecue sausages.

Break beef into bite-sized pieces and cut sausages into ½-inch slices; add both to beans. Stir in all remaining ingredients except flour. Simmer until beans are tender.

When beans are practically done (normally after about 3 to 4 hours total cooking time), taste and add more salt and chile con carne seasoning as desired. Remove small amount of liquid and mix flour into it as you do when making gravy. Add flour mixture to beans and simmer for a final 30 minutes. Makes 20 or more servings.

Serve with a green salad and French bread. Follow with a dessert made by mixing slightly melted vanilla ice cream with partially set strawberry-flavored gelatin, then letting the mixture harden in the refrigerator.

Fried Green Tomatoes

You don't have to have your own tomatoes if you can find a grower, as Dan Cota did. He reports: "Once, to my surprise and delight, I found a field of tomato plants, and asked for a few green ones. The man thought I was drunk or crazy until someone else said, 'Haven't you ever eaten fried green tomatoes?'

"As I prepare them they are delicious hot or cold, as a vegetable or appetizer. Even our dachshunds love them once the sour cream is on."

4 green tomatoes (no color showing,
2½ to 4 inches in diameter)
About ½ cup flour
1 egg, well beaten
2 tablespoons water
1 teaspoon salt
⅛ teaspoon pepper
¼ teaspoon Worcestershire
¼ teaspoon crushed basil
About 1 cup cracker crumbs
2 tablespoons salad oil
2 tablespoons butter
About 1 cup commerical sour cream

Core tomatoes and cut a thin slice off both ends. Cut into ½-inch slices and dust lightly with flour on both sides. Beat egg with water, salt, pepper, Worcestershire, and basil, and dip flour-coated slices into egg mixture. Coat well with crushed cracker crumbs. Heat salad oil and butter in a frying pan; sauté tomato slices until browned on both sides. Drain on paper towels. Top each slice with sour cream. Makes 4 servings.

Asparagus Supreme

Garfield Quimby has hit on a combination of asparagus, mushrooms, and soy sauce that seems so inevitable that you wonder why it isn't used much more widely. It suggests Oriental food, but an Oriental dish would probably include some thinly sliced meat. Come to think of it, an addition of meat would be fine if you ever feel like experimenting with this dish.

1 pound fresh asparagus
1 can (2 or 3 oz.) sliced mushrooms
Water
½ teaspoon cornstarch
1 tablespoon salad oil
½ teaspoon salt
½ teaspoon monosodium glutamate
1 teaspoon soy sauce

Select fresh, tender, plump spears of asparagus. Wash and break off woody parts. Place spears on cutting board and slice on a diagonal into thin slices about 3/16 inch thick. Drain mushrooms and save the liquid. Add enough water to liquid to make ½ cup, then add the cornstarch, stirring until dissolved.

Place salad oil in a hot frying pan; add the asparagus and stir to coat all pieces evenly. Add salt and monosodium glutamate; cook for 4 minutes, stirring, then add the cornstarch dissolved in liquid, the mushrooms, and soy sauce. Heat quickly to the boiling point. Serve immediately. Makes 2 or 3 servings.

ᗯᗯ More or Less Baked Zucchini ᗯᗯ

If it's getting to the end of home-garden zucchini season and your enthusiasm for these vegetables has waned a bit, some of those still on your vines may have become overgrown monsters.

Help is at hand. Frank R. Brown says, "This is a basic recipe for baked zucchini squash. The only difficulty being that you must either grow the squash or have a friend who does, since you need one 10 to 12 inches long, more or less. So the first step is to get the squash.

"A point of interest: If skin on squash can easily be cut with a fingernail, do not remove seeds; they will cook tender and tasty. If skin is tough, remove seeds.

"Around here we call this 'the more or less' baked zucchini. You can add more of your favorite seasonings and less of the others. Also you'll find you will eat more of this and less of something else."

**1 large zucchini, 10-12 inches long
for every 3 or 4 persons**

BASIC STUFFING MIXTURE (each zucchini)

**1 lump of soft butter or margarine about the
size of a walnut (about 2 tablespoons)
¼ teaspoon garlic powder, or to taste
1 tablespoon prepared mustard
1 teaspoon salt, or to taste
(less if bacon is used)
⅛ teaspoon pepper, or to taste
Parmesan cheese or 2 to 3 slices
cooked and crumbled bacon**

Cut the zucchini in half the long way. Score the halves in both directions, but be careful not to cut through the skin. Blend together the butter or margarine, garlic powder, mustard, salt, and pepper. Force this mixture into the cuts in the zucchini. Place in a baking pan with enough water to cover the bottom.

Cover with foil and bake in a moderate oven (350°) for 40 minutes. Remove and take off the foil, sprinkle with Parmesan cheese or crumbled bacon, and put back into oven just long enough to heat either the cheese or bacon.

Serve immediately so zucchini will be hot.

❦ Pimientos and Mushrooms ❦

Mushrooms seem to be showing up more and more frequently in the dishes eaten these days. In addition to providing worthwhile substance in themselves, they have almost magical efficacy in transforming a relatively ordinary dish into something very special. You might serve Robert E. Beckett's recipe as a salad first course.

1 can (4 oz.) whole pimientos
2 cups (about 16) sliced raw mushrooms
½ cup olive oil
¼ cup basil-flavored white wine vinegar
½ teaspoon basil
½ teaspoon salt
1 tablespoon dry white wine
Lettuce

Drain pimientos; cut each in 6 to 8 pieces. Combine pimientos, and mushrooms in a deep bowl. Blend oil, vinegar, basil, salt, and wine in a pint jar. Shake well. Pour over pimientos and mushrooms. Cover and marinate at room temperature 2 to 3 hours. Remove from marinade (save for judicious use in a green salad dressing later). Arrange crisp lettuce leaves on a serving platter, top with mixture of pimientos and mushrooms. Makes 6 servings.

❦ Adventuresome Curried Bananas ❦

Some people feel that bananas are good only when eaten out-of-hand, with a short, unpeeled section serving as a handle. Others admit that they're not bad sliced into a cream pie. Colonel E. Jeff Barnette belongs to a third, more adventurous group. Here he cooks up his bananas in a sweetened, curry-flavored mixture that makes them suitable to accompany game, ham, pork, or poultry, in lieu of a vegetable.

½ cup orange juice
½ cup dry white wine
½ cup light brown sugar, firmly packed
3 tablespoons melted butter
2 tablespoons lemon juice
¾ teaspoon curry powder
4 to 6 large, green-tipped bananas, peeled and
cut in half lengthwise

Combine orange juice, wine, brown sugar, butter, lemon juice, and curry powder in a small pan and simmer until fluid is syrupy (about one third original volume). Arrange halved bananas in a buttered 9 by 13-inch, shallow baking dish leaving space between the halves. Pour on the reduced sauce and bake, uncovered, in a moderate oven (350°) for 20 minutes, basting frequently. Makes about 6 servings.

⚛ Mushroom-Oyster Bake ⚛

"Delightful spring rains had the mushrooms sprouting all over my ranch," says Franz R. Sachse, "and having picked a couple of bucketfuls of beauties, I decided to experiment. The result is Mushroom-Oyster Bake. I don't think that there anything unique about baked mushrooms and oysters, but the sauce is my own production."

Raw oyster fans may take it or leave it, but this dish is a delightful surprise.

1 dozen large mushrooms
(1½ to 2 inches in diameter)
½ cup (1 cube) butter
2 cups cut-up mushrooms and stems
1 can (2 oz.) anchovy fillets
¼ teaspoon liquid hot-pepper seasoning
12 large oysters
1 teaspoon chopped fresh parsley

Cut off mushroom stems and save. Sauté mushroom caps 3 to 4 minutes in butter. Remove to a well greased cooky sheet. Chop mushroom stems and enough additional whole mushrooms for a total of about 2 cups. Sauté in the same skillet until limp and brown. Chop anchovies or cut with scissors into small pieces; add to mushroom stems along with oil from the can. Add liquid hot-pepper seasoning and simmer over very low heat.

Meanwhile plunk a large oyster on each of the mushroom caps and season with paprika. Put into a moderate oven (350°) for about 10 to 12 minutes. Remove, spoon over sauce from skillet, sprinkle with chopped parsley, and serve. Makes 4 servings.

⚛ Sesame Summer Squash ⚛

"Summer is coming down the pike once again, and I am doing likewise with a recipe for a vegetable that's very uninteresting when taken by itself, alone and unadorned: the summer squash."

Just a minute, George J. Watkins: Some insist it never tastes better than when cooked plain and seasoned only with butter, salt, and pepper. All right, if you're one of these, and think you have eaten your fill of it summer-fresh, you'll accept this as a very good variation.

2½ pounds summer squash
1 clove garlic
Water
2 tablespoons sesame seed
⅔ cup sharp Cheddar cheese
Salt to taste

Stem and wash summer squash, slice thin, and place in large frying pan. Squeeze the clove of garlic over the top, add just enough water so squash will steam tender with a lid on, and place over heat. In separate small frying pan, toss sesame seed, shaking over heat until deep brown; set aside. Shred cheese. When squash is cooked, drain off remaining water, then mash with a fork. Salt to taste, add sesame seed and cheese. Stir well and place over heat, covered, until cheese melts and blends. Makes 6 servings.

⚛ Surfers' Hangtown Fry ⚛

"After a day of surfing," says W. E. Gish, "I'm often drafted as chef of the 'surfboard set'. This variation of Hangtown Fry makes an unusual plate-sized serving and a very pleasant surfing supper."

This furnishes an unusual use for eggplant. If you don't care for eggplant, the remaining ingredients would go well on toast or on English muffins.

> 1 large eggplant
> 2 slightly beaten eggs
> 1½ cups fine dry bread crumbs
> Melted shortening or butter
> 6 eggs
> ¼ cup cream or half-and-half
> (half cream, half milk)
> 2 tablespoons sherry
> 1 pint oysters, coarsely chopped
> Salt to taste
> Pepper to taste
> Butter
> ½ pound Cheddar cheese, sliced

Slice eggplant into 8 slices about ¼-inch thick, discarding the end pieces. Dip the slices into the slightly beaten eggs, then into the bread crumbs. Fry in melted shortening (or equal parts shortening and butter) or broil until crisp and brown on both sides.

Beat the 6 eggs with the cream; add sherry, oysters, salt, and pepper, and heat in butter over medium heat. Place mounds of this mixture on eggplant slices and cover each with sliced cheese. Broil until cheese melts, forming a blanket. Makes 4 servings.

Little niceties like chives, crisp bacon, or mushrooms may be added to the basic mixture if desired.

⚛ Barbecued Corn on the Cob ⚛

Says George Morris, "There are many ways to barbecue corn on the cob. I have used various vegetables (tomatoes, squash, onions, etc.) inside the husks for added moisture and flavor. But the most successful are bean sprouts."

Bean sprouts add only the mildest of flavors, but their water content keeps this corn as moist as any you've ever eaten.

Husk corn and save the husks. Wash corn, spread with oil or butter, and season with salt and pepper. Set each ear back inside its husk—and just before closing —spread about ½ cup bean sprouts along its length. Then wrap husk around corn, enclose in double thickness of foil, and grill about 6 inches above coals for 12 to 15 minutes, turning two or three times. Serve with or without the husks, according to the spirit of the occasion.

If grill space is crowded, put two ears of corn in each wrapping of foil.

Dolmades with Avgolemono Sauce

Of course, the original edible wrapper was probably some form of leaf. A close equivalent is the so-called "leaf" of a cabbage, used extensively for this purpose in Greek cookery. Angelos Theodos' recipe presents a good example of a leaf-wrapped dish. The flavoring is subtle and unusual; it's not often that you see cinnamon and oregano used together.

1 large head cabbage
Boiling salted water
1 pound ground beef (or ½ pound ground
beef and ½ pound ground lamb)
2 small onions, chopped
1 cup uncooked rice
1 egg, slightly beaten
½ teaspoon cinnamon
Dash oregano
Salt to taste
Pepper to taste
½ cup (1 cube) butter

Separate cabbage leaves and remove hard core; cook leaves in boiling salted water until slightly tender. Remove cabbage and save 1½ cups of the cooking water. Mix meat with onions, rice, egg, seasonings, and ½ cup of the cooking water to make filling. Place a little of the filling in the center of a cabbage leaf, roll it up, and place in saucepan. Continue until all filling is used up. Cut up any remaining cabbage and arrange on top of rolls. Dot with butter. Add 1 cup of the water in which the cabbage cooked. Place a heat-proof plate over the rolls; cover the pan and cook 35 to 45 minutes, or until rice is tender. Serve with the special sauce made as follows:

Avgolemono Sauce

Beat 1 egg with 2 teaspoons water until light and fluffy. Add a little broth from food on which it is to be used; continue beating. When light and foamy, pour in juice of ½ lemon. Stir well.

Pour Avgolemono Sauce over the Dolmades and serve. Makes about 14 rolls (4 to 6 servings).

ꙮ Champignons aux Fines Herbes ꙮ

Halsey Stevens, a composer and a professor of music, is also a composer of unique and subtle recipes.

"I often find that a recipe sets the imagination—and the taste buds—off exploring at a tangent. This is what happened here: A delicious recipe for 'Parisian Mushrooms' provided by one of my students stimulated the development of this dish—which is totally unlike it. The seasoning may need modification, since the proportions are based upon the use of a specific kind of seasoned salt and a specific mixture of fines herbes (mine includes thyme, oregano, sage, rosemary, marjoram, and sweet basil)."

This very herby side dish should make an excellent accompaniment for barbecued red meat of robust character.

> ½ pound medium to large fresh mushrooms
> ½ teaspoon seasoned salt
> ½ teaspoon fines herbs
> ¼ teaspoon dry mustard
> 2 tablespoons butter
> 1 tablespoon red wine vinegar

Wash and dry mushrooms, cut off ends of stems without separating them from the caps, and slice ⅛-inch thick (center slices will look like capitals of Ionic columns). Sprinkle with seasoning salt, fines herbes, and dry mustard. Brown in butter, adding more if necessary to keep mushrooms moist. When nearly done, add vinegar; reheat, and serve hot. Makes about 4 servings as a side dish.

ꙮ Danish Sauerkraut ꙮ

Pork, sauerkraut, and pineapple make a good sweet-and-sour triangle. But some like it more sauer than others, and some are specially insistent about making sure that it includes plenty of meat. Both these controversies indicate how you may want to vary the proportions in what Niels Paulsen calls Danish Sauerkraut so that it will exactly suit your taste. If you find the combination a little too sweet, for example, you might cut back somewhat on the pineapple.

> 2 to 6 fresh pork hocks
> 1 large can (1 lb., 12 oz.) sauerkraut
> 1 small can (8½ oz.) crushed pineapple
> 1 large onion, minced
> 1 large teaspoon freshly ground pepper
> ½ cup water

Have meatman saw each pork hock into 2 or 3 pieces. Wash them and put in large kettle with cover. Add sauerkraut, pineapple, onion, and pepper. Rinse out kraut and pineapple cans with the water and add to kettle. Cover and cook over medium heat until meat is tender, about 3 hours. Serve as a main dish for lunch or light supper, or a side dish for dinner. Makes 4 to 6 servings.

⚛ Cabbage Plus ⚛

A winter standby in the days of home storehouses was cabbage. Cabbage appeared as sauerkraut; cabbage was served with corned beef; cabbage took its part in the boiled dinner. Although the cabbage has by no means disappeared, it sometimes meets with objections nowadays on the grounds of its virile odor once cooked.

James Helmer offers a simple suggestion which helps to mask the odor, producing cabbage that smells spicy and delicious. He says, "I found that cabbage did not go over very well with the children, so decided to cook it with a little imagination. The spices and vinegar give it a certain dash that ordinary cabbage lacks."

1 teaspoon whole mixed pickling spice
¼ cup garlic-flavored wine vinegar
1 teaspoon salt
¼ teaspoon pepper
1 medium-sized head cabbage, finely shredded
3 tablespoons butter

Fill a pan with enough water to cover cabbage. Add spice, vinegar, salt and pepper; bring to a boil. Add cabbage and cook just until tender, about 3 to 5 minutes. Drain, and add butter. Makes 8 servings.

⚛ Sour Cream Brussels Sprouts ⚛

Palmer Field submits a family favorite—"a very simple and completely delicious hot vegetable dish for any dinner menu."

The dish is good-looking, with the pale green and dark green contrast of spinach and sprouts. Sour cream ties their flavors together. In fact, it might even convert a few of the fastidious who usually turn up their noses at Brussels sprouts.

One very important point should be noted: After cooking the Brussels sprouts, you have to let them cool. Then you cut them up, combine with creamed spinach, and reheat. If the sprouts are cooked too long the first time, they are mushy when finally served. So *don't overcook* on the first round.

1½ pounds fresh Brussels sprouts
1 package (about 10 oz.) spinach
frozen in cream sauce
1 tablespoon butter
½ pint commercial sour cream
Salt to taste
Pepper to taste

Trim any wilted leaves or woody sections of stem from the Brussels sprouts. Put in a steamer over boiling water and cook until barely tender crisp but still firm —about 20 minutes. Cool. Cook creamed spinach according to package directions. Meanwhile, melt butter in a casserole dish and coat the bottom and sides.

When the sprouts have cooled enough to handle, cut each in half and place in casserole. Pour creamed spinach and sour cream over sprouts and gently fold all together. Season to taste. Cover casserole and place in a 350° oven to warm.

Makes 6 to 8 servings.

⚒ Steamed-Stuffed Onions ⚒

"The only potentially difficult part in cooking my Steamed-Stuffed Onions," says Jerry Whalen, "is the steaming—and steamed they must be, never actually boiled in water. I don't have a large steamer, so I prop the meat rack of my Dutch oven up on jar lids to keep it above the level of the boiling water."

Jerry's dish uses the traditional Creole flavoring and thickening agent called "filé" (pronounced *fee-lay*), which is available on the spice shelf of most markets.

6 medium-large onions
Salt to taste
Pepper to taste

STUFFING

1 cup prepared poultry dressing
¼ cup white wine (more, if necessary, to moisten stuffing thoroughly)
½ teaspoon gumbo filé
About 2 tablespoons slivered blanched almonds
Salt to taste
Freshly ground pepper to taste
Butter
Chopped parsley

Select firm onions (red, white, or yellow are equally satisfactory). Slice off top of each onion and peel carefully; don't cut across the root end. Scoop out center rings of the onion, leaving at least two of the outer rings intact (cut an X through the interior rings with the tip of a sharp knife to ease the job). Salt and pepper onions lightly; steam gently for 15 minutes while you prepare the stuffing.

Mix together all remaining ingredients except butter and parsley. Remove onions from steamer and drain water out of cavities, then stuff with dressing, dot top with butter, and sprinkle with chopped parsley. Return onions to steamer and steam for another 10 minutes, or until properly done. Watch carefully during final steaming; onions should be *al dente* or tender-crisp, never soft and mushy. Serve hot. Makes 6 servings as a side dish.

These onions go well with grilled or roasted meats and, surprisingly, very well indeed with broiled or baked chicken.

⚞ Turnip Hopeful ⚟

"We had been expecting a visit from Pappy Yocum and he did not show up," relates R. O. Lamb. "We had laid in a stock of turnips, so what to do with 'ugh' the turnips?

"Nachally a normal person might throw them away, but being of rugged pioneer stock, I insisted something had to be done with them. Here is my recipe for Turnip Hopeful. It tastes far better than just turnips."

1 large bunch turnips
1 egg
½ cup milk
½ cup shredded Cheddar cheese
3 tablespoons wheat germ
1 teaspoon Worcestershire
1 tablespoon finely minced onion
1 tablespoon minced parsley
Salt to taste
Pepper to taste

TOPPING

¼ cup crushed round salted crackers
2 tablespoons shredded Cheddar cheese
1 tablespoon butter

Peel and cook turnips; when soft enough, put through food mill or potato ricer until they are rather smooth in consistency. Beat an egg and add to turnips with all remaining ingredients. Turn into greased 1-quart baking dish and top with crushed crackers that have been mixed with cheese and butter. Bake in slow oven (350°) until heated through, about 20 minutes. Makes 4 servings.

⚞ Corn in its Own Coat ⚟

"Never, never boil an ear of corn." General F. E. Calhoun says it rather dogmatically. "There is really only one way to prepare corn on the cob—cook it in nature's very own wrappings."

But the follow-through on Calhoun Corn is how you cook it to keep it moist, tender, fresh tasting, and not burned on the ends the way it gets when you throw it on the coals.

By the "Braille method," select untrimmed and "un-windowed" corn (no holes or slashes in the husk). Snip off silk end and remove one layer of the husk. Place on racks of oven, preheated to very hot (500° to 550°). After 12 minutes, remove ears, husk (wearing barbecue mittens), butter, and eat. Prepare to repeat several times.

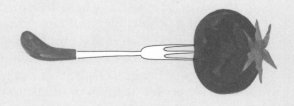

TOSS A MEAN SALAD

Green salads, unlike green vegetables, have always had status. This has been particularly true on the Pacific Coast, where green salads were introduced by early immigrants from France and Italy. The custom of serving such a salad as a separate first course, or with the meal, is now widespread in this country. But new twists within the basic formulas still originate in the West, where lettuce, avocados, artichokes, oranges, grapefruit, and lemons are especially plentiful most of the year.

Some of the recipes in this chapter give explicit directions as to the kinds of salad greens to put into a salad bowl as well as definite instructions on tossing, mixing, or arranging them. Some of the recipes are for dressings, leaving the choice of greens up to you. There are also recipes for other kinds of salads, calling for other ingredients, such as potatoes, asparagus, celery root, zucchini, crab, shrimp, and even turnips.

☇ Coddled Egg Caesar Salad ☇

Here is a Caesar Salad, but it has been modified to Lawrence LeClaire's taste. The egg is coddled (one-minute-boiled rather than raw), bacon replaces anchovy, and other ingredients vary in small ways from the standard recipe.

1 head romaine lettuce
½ teaspoon salt (or garlic salt)
½ teaspoon freshly ground pepper
¼ teaspoon dry mustard
¼ cup olive oil
1 teaspoon fresh lemon juice
2 tablespoons red wine vinegar
½ cup garlic croutons
3 slices bacon, fried crisp and broken into small pieces
¼ cup Parmesan cheese
1 coddled egg, mixed with rotary beater

Tear leaves of romaine from head and wash in warm water; drain thoroughly. Place in a large bowl, cover, and place in refrigerator for 2 hours (lettuce will become very crisp). Remove from bowl; shake any remaining moisture from each leaf. Take outside leaves and tear leaf from its stalk in sections approximately 2 inches square, then discard stalks. Tear center leaves but retain the stalks (they add sweetness).

Place lettuce in salad bowl, add salt and pepper, and toss. Sprinkle with dry mustard and toss again. Pour in olive oil and toss again, making sure lettuce is completely covered with oil. Add lemon juice and vinegar; toss again. Add croutons, bacon, and Parmesan cheese; toss. Pour in coddled egg and toss for final blessing. Serve immediately.

Makes 3 servings.

☇ Romaine Romano ☇

F. E. C. Hilliard carefully hedges his claim: "This may not be an original invention, but it is new to me and my own little concoction as far as I am concerned."

It is an arrangement of salad ingredients, put together with very much of an eye for decorative effect, yet not neglecting to make it a very pleasing food composition.

1 medium-sized head romaine lettuce
1 tablespoon olive oil
1 tablespoon basil wine vinegar
½ cup small curd cottage cheese
1 medium-sized avocado
2 tablespoons sliced green onion tops
¼ cup julienne strips of sour pickle
¼ cup pitted black olives
1 large hard-cooked egg
Salt
Pepper

Take off the tender romaine leaves and cut the center stalk out of each leaf. Moisten with olive oil and vinegar and arrange the broken leaves on a salad plate. Place cottage cheese on the greens. Peel, seed, and dice avocado and place pieces close together on the cheese. Scatter sliced green onion over. Garnish with sour pickle, olive, and egg (cut into eighths and salted and peppered). Makes 4 servings.

◈ Oranges Companionable ◈

Among the merits of this outstanding recipe from Jerry Whalen is the fact that it provides an excellent use for capers. And of course, there is always a demand for good, simple side dishes to serve with barbecued meats.

Jerry barbecues often. "Of late, charcoal consumption has more than doubled at our house. At this rate my near neighbors are likely to mark the period as the Year of the Big Smoke! I submit for consideration a citrus salad that goes happily with barbecues of beef, pork, lamb, and poultry."

4 large oranges
2 firm-ripe avocados
2 to 4 tablespoons honey, according to taste
4 tablespoons tarragon wine vinegar
Salt
Lemon juice
4 tablespoons capers

Chill oranges and avocados until serving time. Blend honey and tarragon vinegar. Peel oranges and cut into bite-sized chunks, removing seeds and as much of the white membrane as possible. Peel avocados and cut into chunks; sprinkle with salt and lemon juice to retard discoloration. Combine orange and avocado chunks and toss gently. Heap onto crisp greens or serve in footed seafood cocktail glasses. Dribble honey-vinegar dressing over each serving and garnish with drained capers. Makes 4 servings.

◈ Sur-Prized Salad ◈

Cooking takes a certain amount of basic knowledge, but some of the best recipes are the result of happy accident. (The unhappy ones end quietly in the garbage.) Glenn Jensen tells how one of these accidents came about.

"I saw some diced, boiled potatoes in the refrigerator, and thought I'd make up a potato salad. I was putting the finishing touches to it when, lo and behold, my wife walked in and said, 'Those were turnips!' A neighbor dropped in at that point, and we offered her some without comment. She said: 'How delicious. What kind of potatoes did you use?' Together we finished up the whole batch."

2 bunches turnips (about 4½ lbs.)
Boiling, salted water
6 hard-cooked eggs
¼ cup chopped onion
2 cups sliced celery
1 cup mayonnaise
1 teaspoon prepared mustard
Salt
Pepper

Peel turnips and cook in boiling, salted water until done but still firm, refrigerate until thoroughly cold, and cut in 1-inch cubes. (You should have about 5 cups.) Chop 5 eggs and add to turnips, reserving an egg for garnish. Add the onion, celery, the mayonnaise blended with mustard, and salt and pepper to taste. Mix well, and garnish with slices of egg. Makes about 8 servings.

〰 Colorful Potato Salad 〰

A good potato salad, eaten in a shady spot on a hot summer's day, never fails to please. You can't expect gasps of surprise, but you nearly always get murmurs of pleasure.

Most of us have an old favorite mixture that comes out lumpy and good in a large bowl and disappears rapidly. Stuart B. Moseley proposes a few additions that add color and flavor so as to spark the eye as well as the appetite. It's the olives, he says, that make all the difference.

3 medium-sized potatoes, boiled, peeled, and cubed
3 hard-cooked eggs, sliced or chopped
2 stalks celery, thinly sliced
1 medium-sized onion, chopped
1 jar (2 oz.) pimiento, drained and chopped
1 jar (2 oz.) stuffed green olives, drained and sliced thin
2 tablespoons sweet pickle relish
4 tablespoons chopped green pepper
¾ cup mayonnaise
2 tablespoons vinegar
1 tablespoon prepared mustard
¼ teaspoon dill seed, optional
¼ teaspoon sage, optional
1½ teaspoons seasoned salt
1 tablespoon parsley flakes

Combine potatoes, eggs, celery, onion, pimiento, olives, relish, and green pepper in a bowl. Mix mayonnaise, vinegar, mustard, dill seed and sage (if used), seasoned salt, and parsley flakes, and pour over potato salad mixture. Mix lightly. Makes 6 to 8 servings.

〰 Copenhagen Cucumbers 〰

When cucumbers are a-coming in, try them once in this dish that A. L. Marshall calls Copenhagen Cucumbers. It's one of many versions of "pressed cucumbers," but it's a good one, especially if you alternate bites of this with bites of some meat or casserole dish that is pretty rich by comparison.

2 cucumbers
Salt
2 teaspoons sugar
¼ cup vinegar

Peel cucumbers and cut into slices about the thickness of a dime—the thinner the better. Spread out slices on a board and sprinkle with salt. After about 15 minutes, squeeze out all the liquid you can from cucumbers. (Do this by taking palmfuls of the slices, keeping them flat, and squeezing them between your hands.) Put the alarmingly limp slices in a bowl, sprinkle with sugar, and barely cover with vinegar. In another 15 minutes they are ready. They will have a crackling consistency. Makes 6 servings.

⚘ Main-Dish Salad ⚘

"We Hambergers are very fond of celery root, and use it in many different ways, but we like it particularly well in a salad," says Maurice T. Hamberger.

Just reading the list of ingredients may make you smack your lips. Because so many of these things are rich, hearty, and expensive, we'd recommend serving this salad as a main dish with simple accompaniments—French bread or bread sticks and a chilled white wine.

> 2 bouillon cubes
> 2 cups water
> 2 medium-sized celery roots, peeled
> 1 package (8 oz.) frozen artichoke hearts
> ½ pound small shrimp, either fresh
>   or fresh frozen
> ½ pound crab meat, either fresh
>   or fresh frozen
> 1 cup Louis dressing (recipe follows)
> Lettuce
> 2 medium-sized avocados, peeled
> 2 hard-cooked eggs, sliced
> 1 small can (about 4 oz.) pitted black olives
> 1 small can (2 oz.) sliced pimiento

Add bouillon cubes to water; heat to boiling, stirring until bouillon is dissolved. Add celery roots and parboil until just done enough to pierce with a fork (too much cooking makes them mushy). Drain and chill. Cook frozen artichoke hearts according to package directions.

Dice the celery root, and put in a large bowl. Add shrimp, crab meat, and artichoke hearts, and mix well. Add half the dressing and stir again thoroughly.

Arrange lettuce in the bottom of a salad bowl or serving dish. Mound celery root-shrimp-crab mixture in center. Around it arrange slices of avocado, hard-cooked egg, and pitted olive. Place bits of pimiento in the holes in the olive slices. Serve remaining dressing in a bowl. Serve each person some extra dressing along with his portion of salad. Makes 4 to 6 servings.

Louis Dressing

Combine 1 cup mayonnaise, ½ cup chile sauce, ½ teaspoon Worcestershire, and dash liquid hot-pepper seasoning; mix until well blended.

☗ Salad Virtuoso ☗

Karl W. Hinkle offers this salad with a preamble: "When I was a small boy in Iowa, the first salad greens my family had in the spring were fresh wild dandelions. And over these my mother served a sour cream, cider vinegar, sweetened dressing.

"Since the dandelion of Midwestern succulence is not available in the West, I could never attempt to reproduce the salad of my boyhood. But memories have encouraged repeated experimentation toward a salad I might like as well. Out of these attempts over the years has come a very different salad and dressing, a combination that satisfies the 'inner man' as did the dandelion salad that once satisfied the 'inner boy'. It seems to go well with equal proportions head lettuce, romaine, and chicory."

2 quarts salad greens
6 strips bacon
2 to 4 tablespoons wine vinegar
¾ teaspoon salt
1½ tablespoons raw or brown sugar
½ teaspoon prepared mustard
1 teaspoon prepared horseradish (optional)
¼ cup evaporated milk
Dash Angostura bitters
2 small green onions, chopped fine, or 1 clove
garlic put through garlic press
2 hard-cooked eggs, diced
1 small avocado, quartered and sliced
2 ounces Roquefort cheese, crumbled

Wash greens, shake dry, break up into bite-sized pieces, and place in refrigerator to chill. Cut bacon into ½-inch squares and fry slowly until crisp but not overly brown. To the vinegar add the salt, sugar, mustard, and horseradish. Stir until well dissolved. Add evaporated milk and stir again. Add bacon squares, bitters and chopped green onions or garlic.

Just before serving salad, toss greens in dressing, making sure the bacon is well distributed. Add hard-cooked eggs, avocado, and Roquefort. Toss these in lightly, since they are somewhat soft and fragile. Several sprigs of fresh dill could be added, if you wish, to furnish the final master touch.

Makes 4 to 8 servings.

☗ Simplicity Avocado Dressing ☗

"This is a simple dressing for avocado on the half shell that has been used in our family ever since I can remember," says Terry T. Hayashi. "Our friends who have tasted it all seem to like its very refreshing taste as contrasted with the richness of the avocado."

2 tablespoons sugar
¼ cup boiling water
2 tablespoons cider vinegar
1 tablespoon soy sauce

Dissolve sugar in water; add vinegar and soy sauce. Chill. Pour into avocado halves just before serving. Makes enough sauce for 6 or 8 avocado halves.

⚹ The Chutney Caper ⚹

Mort Greene submits a recipe that recalls the dear, dead days of radio drama; specifically detective Sam Spade. The name of his mysterious recipe is The Chutney Caper. The connection is not too surprising, since Mort works with a television network.

The mystery dressing is slightly sweet, and is intended for fruit salad, or for slices of avocado and grapefruit sections; but once you have tried it, you may find that you'll like it with seafood or with iceberg lettuce just as well.

1 cup mayonnaise
⅓ cup commercial sour cream
2 tablespoons chutney
1 tablespoon capers
2 tablespoons chopped chives
1 tablespoon sliced pimiento
¼ teaspoon curry powder (or more to taste)
2 tablespoons sherry

Blend ingredients well, and serve with fresh fruit salad, avocado and grapefruit salad, or iceberg lettuce. Makes about 2 cups dressing.

⚹ Sparrowgrass Green Salad ⚹

Hugh Paradise seeks food adventures in the course of all his travels: "In the lower Yakima Valley of Washington, asparagus readily escapes from cultivation. So roadsides are sometimes regular asparagus patches, with the slender tips poking up as thick as grass. These "wild" spears seem much tastier than those from the private side of the fence; and, since they are the prime first picking, no doubt are really asparagus at its best.

"One thing we learned, out there where it was difficult to keep it unwilted for very long in the valley's heat, was how delicious raw asparagus is. Once we discovered this, we simply chopped the tender sprouts right into our tossed noon salad and ate something really special."

If it's too late to enjoy picking asparagus wild, and if the domesticated version is plentiful in markets, there's no point in saving this good recipe for another season.

About 1½ pounds fresh asparagus
(about 4 cups when sliced)
About 6 cups lettuce (your choice of type),
in bite-sized pieces
About ½ cup Roquefort-type salad dressing

Remove the tougher bottom ends of the asparagus; cut the tender sections on the diagonal into thin slices. Combine asparagus and lettuce in a salad bowl and pour over salad dressing (thinned with oil and vinegar, if necessary, to keep it from being too thick and heavy). Toss and serve. Makes 6 to 8 servings.

⚹ Greenstuff Salad ⚹

Very often the important part of a green salad recipe is the dressing, and you have considerable latitude in choice of greens. But here the reverse is true.

Vic Destin's choice of greens is not nearly as miscellaneous as it might appear. On tasting (and chewing), you discover a good balance of the various sharp and bland, crisp and soft, large and small ingredients. Go easy on the dressing for this salad; the aim is to coat it evenly, not to drown it.

1 head romaine lettuce, broken into
bite-sized pieces
1 head red-leaf lettuce, broken into
bite-sized pieces
½ green pepper, sliced into strips
about ¼-inch wide
6 to 8 green onions, cut into ¼-inch slices
6 to 8 radishes, sliced thin
1 cucumber, peeled and sliced thin
Dash of coarse-ground pepper
Pinch thyme
Pinch tarragon
1 to 2 ounces blue cheese (or Roquefort), crumbled
2 slices toasted bread, diced
1 avocado
Pinch of salt, or to taste
6 to 8 tablespoons prepared or homemade
oil-and-vinegar dressing

Combine all ingredients except avocado, salt, and dressing, putting the cheese and diced toast on top. Chill. Just before serving, slice avocado and add. Add salt and dressing, toss, and serve immediately. Makes 6 to 8 servings.

Fresh shrimp may also be added.

⚹ Short-Time Roquefort Dressing ⚹

Herbert Auerbach contributes a simple and original blend of flavors. Says he, "I have made many inquiries and a diligent search for a simple method of preparing a cheese dressing. I give you this recipe; note that the seasonings are few and time of preparation short."

1 small package (3 oz.) Roquefort cheese
1 tablespoon warm water
1 teaspoon Worcestershire
⅛ teaspoon garlic salt
1 cup mayonnaise
½ cup sherry
1 tablespoon white or herb-flavored vinegar
½ teaspoon salt
⅛ teaspoon pepper

Have cheese at room temperature. Break into small pieces, add the warm water and Worcestershire, and use a spoon to mash cheese to a paste. Add other ingredients in order, beating until well blended. Before using, keep for a day in the refrigerator, after which a decided improvement will be noted—all ingredients will be blended and adding to each other. Makes almost 1 pint of dressing.

❧ Leeky Lemon Dressing ❧

That "fresh taste" will tantalize your taste buds when you sample this salad dressing. It is rather bland (also blond), more so than the usual oil and vinegar type of dressing. Thus it is best with fish and fowl entrées that can do with some lightly flavored greens on the side.

According to John S. Burke, "This new formula has been well received not only by the eight Burkes but by several other families and individual testers."

1 medium-sized leek (or about 5 green onions), trimmed and sliced
8 pickled cocktail onions
Juice of 2 lemons
About 1/5 the outer rind of a lemon, sliced
1 piece of garlic approximately the size of ¼-inch cube
1 teaspoon sugar
⅓ teaspoon pepper
1 cup salad oil
1 egg

Place all ingredients except oil and egg into blender and run until ground fine. While blender is still operating, add oil, then egg. When well mixed, remove to refrigerator and chill. Serve on tossed green salad. Makes enough dressing for about three salads, each serving 8. Keeps well under refrigeration.

❧ Gourmet Dressing for Fatties ❧

Good news for dieters is always welcome during these days of slimming one's way to good health. Like a good cook should in these circumstances, Chester James Small sets his sights high; he created this salad dressing "for gourmets," no less. He says it is low-fat and remains fluffy and good for a week in the refrigerator. You might try it also as a dip for chips or crackers.

1 pint cottage cheese
½ pint plain yogurt
Dash garlic powder
Dash onion powder
1 teaspoon coarse (kosher-style) salt
About 1 teaspoon mixed fresh herbs, finely chopped
(suggest about ¼ teaspoon each parsley,
lemon thyme, oregano, winter savory, or
others as available—or use about
⅛ teaspoons each of the dried herbs)
3 teaspoons tarragon wine vinegar, or to taste

Put cottage cheese in an electric mixer or blender and beat or blend until smooth. Add yogurt, garlic powder, onion powder, salt, chopped fresh herbs, and wine vinegar. Beat or blend until well blended. Store in refrigerator—it is better the second day. Makes about 2½ cups dressing.

For variety, crumble about ¼ cup Roquefort or blue cheese into about ⅓ of the dressing. Blend well and refrigerate.

Try slicing tiny, unpeeled zucchini paper thin, then marinating 30 minutes in the dressing before adding to a green salad. It tastes like cucumber, only better. Another good occasional salad ingredient is some finely shredded raw Jerusalem artichoke.

❧ Prawn Pink Salad ❧

Louis H. Prince's prawn salad is hearty and a perennial favorite with men. For best appearance, bring salad and dressing to the table separately, then combine them just before serving, or spoon a little dressing over each serving.

1 pound prawns, in the shell
Salted water
1 head lettuce
2 tomatoes
1 large avocado
3 hard-cooked eggs

DRESSING

⅔ cup mayonnaise
⅓ cup catsup
8 drops Worcestershire

Boil prawns in salted water for 5 minutes. Remove shells and tails, devein, and cool.

Tear up lettuce into bite-sized pieces and place on bottom of salad bowl. Cut up prawns and place in layer on top of lettuce. Cut tomatoes and avocado into small pieces (not slices) and place on top of prawns. Cover with sliced hard-cooked eggs and refrigerate. Combine all three ingredients of the dressing and beat with a spoon until mixture is a smooth, even, pinkish-red color. Refrigerate for about an hour to allow flavors to blend. Before serving, add dressing to salad. Makes about 6 servings.

❧ Orange Tomato Dressing ❧

"Using citrus as a seasoning is a natural for us here in the West," says John S. Burke, "and I've been experimenting along these lines. By popular demand of a large group of appreciative connoisseurs (my family of seven), I submit this example of my art."

⅓ cup cider vinegar
¾ teaspoon dry sweet basil
½ teaspoon grated orange peel
1 teaspoon sugar
3 tablespoons chile sauce
¼ teaspoon salt
⅛ teaspoon pepper
½ cup salad oil

Combine all ingredients except oil and mix well. Allow to mellow overnight if possible, but at least an hour. Just before serving, add oil and mix well. Use generously on tossed green salad.

❧ Old Fashioned Potato Salad ❧

Picnics and potato salads are a standard pair, as far as most people are concerned. But it is often forgotten that it's possible to make more than one kind of potato salad. If you have always eaten the type that is very bland, rich, and oily, you may never have eaten the type represented in this recipe from Thomas M. Conrow. It is nippy and tart, a good sharp counterpoint for richness in other foods—such as barbecued meats.

If the vinegar is too strong for you, cut it back a little. But do try to keep the salad overnight before serving, to let the flavors mix thoroughly.

8 medium-sized potatoes, peeled, and
diced in about ½-inch cubes
5 hard-cooked eggs
½ cup (1 cube) butter or margarine, melted
1 cup vinegar
2 teaspoons salt
1 teaspoon dry mustard
1 medium-sized onion, chopped fine
1 teaspoon celery seed

Boil potatoes until just barely tender. While they are boiling, place yolks of hard-cooked eggs in a small bowl; chop the whites and place in a large bowl. Mash the yolks smooth with the melted butter or margarine, ¾ cup of the vinegar, and the salt and mustard. Drain potatoes and place in bowl with the chopped egg white; add the chopped onion and the celery seed.

While potatoes are hot, add liquid egg mixture and stir well. Store overnight in refrigerator. Before serving, moisten with ¼ cup vinegar. Makes 8 servings.

❧ Dill-Clam-Celery Salad ❧

Ed Colby likes to explore the byways of taste and texture when he is dreaming up one of his fanciful concoctions. Bamboo shoots and water chestnuts are among his favorite additions.

This is a special salad (not for every day) with some pretty subtle flavors, to be eaten in small quantities. It is a little like a spoonful of relish served on a lettuce leaf.

2 hearts of celery
1 can (5 oz.) bamboo shoots
2 cans (7½ oz. each) minced clams
2 cans (5 oz. each) water chestnuts
1 cup mayonnaise
Dash of seasoning salt
1 teaspoon dill weed
¼ teaspoon garlic powder
Juice of 1 lime
Lettuce
Paprika

Slice the hearts of celery, including the small yellow leaves, into a wooden chopping bowl. Add the bamboo shoots, sliced, the drained minced clams, and the drained water chestnuts. Chop until all ingredients are well mixed and minced. Add all but last 2 ingredients and mix together. Place in a glass container, cover, and keep in refrigerator overnight to chill thoroughly. To serve, divide mixture into 4 portions, place each on a nest of fresh, green, crisp lettuce, and top with a dash of paprika for color. Makes 4 servings.

BREADS AND SUCH

Serious baking is a little like serious pottery-making. Both require enough dedication and determination to carry you through all the steps before your masterwork goes into the oven—and then the checking and waiting until it is ready to be taken out again.

Fortunately for would-be bakers, there are less complicated forms of baking. These are especially suitable for men, whose kitchen time is usually rather limited.

There are other things that can be made in a bread way without leaning entirely on the staff of life—things such as coffee cake, muffins, sandwiches.

Only one of the recipes here is a regular yeast bread. About half of them, however, are made from a flour-plus-liquid combination falling somewhere in the range between a dough (which is kneaded) and a batter (which is beaten). The remainder are built upon some form of ready-made bread as an ingredient. Two of the latter are rather rare hybrids: Blintzen Con Queso, best explained as a blintz crossed with a taco; and Yankee Pizza, Italian pizza trimmings on a hamburger bun.

❂ Muffins with Crunch ❂

Rare is the male cook who doesn't occasionally rise on a Sunday morning and say to himself, "I'm going to cook something *really great* for breakfast."

And what happens when he finds he is lacking a critical ingredient? Necessity is the mother . . .

"I stumbled on this recipe one day when I was short of flour," says J. A. Young. He substituted bran flakes and the results were excellent. These are cake-like muffins, moist inside, crunchy outside, and they don't crumble, which is no mean trick with bran muffins. You come across the hidden treasures of walnut and raisin as you bite into the center, but the bran flakes contribute an all-pervading nuttiness which extends to the crust as well.

1 egg
¼ cup melted butter (or salad oil)
¼ cup milk
⅓ cup sugar
½ teaspoon salt
2½ teaspoons baking powder
1 cup bran flakes
1 cup unsifted flour
¼ cup chopped walnuts
¼ cup raisins

Beat egg thoroughly in large bowl of electric mixer. Add melted butter, milk, sugar, salt, baking powder, bran flakes, and flour; stir slowly just until well blended. Stir in walnuts and raisins. Spoon into well greased muffin pan, filling cups about ⅔ full. Bake in a hot oven (400°) until golden brown: about 25 minutes for large muffins, 15 to 18 minutes for small ones. Makes 6 large or 12 small muffins.

❂ Mexican Spoon Bread ❂

It's hard to give an appropriately descriptive name to this dish, but it's good. "You can shut your eyes and think you are eating green corn tamales," says F. E. Blacklidge. It's a natural for a brunch, lunch, or late snack with beer.

1 can (1 lb.) cream-style corn
¾ cup milk
⅓ cup melted shortening
2 eggs, slightly beaten
1 cup cornmeal
½ teaspoon soda
1 teaspoon salt
1 can (4 oz.) green chiles, chopped
1½ cups shredded Cheddar cheese

Mix all ingredients except chiles and cheese in order given above (wet ingredients first, then dry ones). Pour half of batter into greased 9 by 9-inch square baking pan and spread with peeled green chiles and half the cheese. Spread remaining batter on top and sprinkle with remaining cheese. Bake 45 minutes in a hot oven (400°). Remove from oven and let it cool just enough to set a little. Makes 8 to 10 servings.

⚬ Coexistence Water Bagels ⚬

In that brief purple period when San Francisco was considered a center of the Beat Generation, one of the beat hangouts in the city's North Beach district was the Co-existence Bagel Shop.

Now there's nothing particularly beat about bagels. But coexistence is something they decidedly deserve.

Bagels are doughnut-shaped rolls, made with a yeast dough much like bread, but prepared and cooked in a special way to give them their distinct, resilient texture, chewiness, and good, wheaty, homemade bread flavor. The perfect, polished bagels from a specialty baker are very good indeed, but some say you just haven't eaten a proper bagel if you have never tried a homemade water bagel hot from the oven and lavishly spread with butter.

Murray Falkin, born and bred in Brooklyn but now a convert to the Northwest, makes bagels for his family. This is his favorite recipe for water bagels, tested and tried over many years.

> 1 package dry yeast
> 1½ cups water
> 3 teaspoons salt
> 3 tablespoons sugar
> 6 cups sifted flour

Dissolve yeast in water, which should be at room temperature. Add salt and sugar and stir until dissolved. Add flour. Knead dough on lightly floured board for 10 minutes. Let rise in greased bowl for 15 minutes.

Punch flat and form square of dough about 1 inch thick. Use a sharp knife to cut into 12 equal strips. Roll each strip between the fingers until it is about ½ inch in diameter. Join ends to form into doughnut shape by either of two methods: Wrap loosely around three fingers, overlap ends a little, and squeeze together; or form on board by overlapping ends and squeezing together with thumb and forefinger. Work each into uniform shape. Cover all with a towel and let rise 20 minutes.

Place 1 gallon of water in a deep pot, add 1 table-spoon sugar, and bring to a boil. Keep water just under the boiling point and add bagels one at a time; cook 4 or 5 at once. They will sink, then come to the top. Simmer each one for 7 minutes, remove from water with a fork, and place on a towel to cool.

Place on ungreased baking sheet, not touching. Bake in medium oven (375°) for 30 to 35 minutes, or until they are brown. Makes 12 bagels each about 4 inches in diameter.

If you can't eat them right from the baking, they may be warmed in foil, split and toasted, or eaten cold. Slice them crosswise to use for sandwiches and then fill with thin corned beef slices, pastrami, or tuna salad. Or eat them the classic way; with cream cheese and *lox* (lightly smoked salmon).

Bread Crumb Pancakes

For a Sunday morning breakfast or a Saturday night dessert, treat yourself to these very delicate pancakes presented by Bud Getschman. There's also a very tasty footnote on "Special Syrup"; don't over look it.

2 cups milk
2 tablespoons butter or margarine
¾ cup fresh bread crumbs
2 eggs, well beaten
⅔ cup flour
4 teaspoons baking powder
¾ teaspoon salt
1½ teaspoons sugar
¼ teaspoon cinnamon
½ teaspoon grated orange peel (optional)

Scald milk and add butter or margarine. Add bread crumbs and let stand until crumbs are very soft. Add beaten eggs. Sift flour, measure, and sift with the baking powder, salt, sugar, and cinnamon, and add to the first mixture. Add orange peel. Bake on pancake griddle and serve with Special Syrup. Makes 24 cakes about 4 inches in diameter.

Special Syrup

Heat about 1½ cups maple syrup and add 3 tablespoons brandy and 2 tablespoons melted butter. Or make your own syrup by using equal parts of brown sugar and white sugar and half as much water as sugar; flavor with vanilla or brandy or a combination of both.

Starving Boy Sandwich

Drive away any famished feelings with what W. W. Williams calls a Starving Boy Sandwich. You may have eaten something like this before. Perhaps it was called a submarine, but it could not have tasted better than this one, with its green pepper, salami, onion, beef, and assorted spicy bits.

1 loaf French bread
⅔ cup chopped celery
1 large onion, chopped
½ cup chopped green pepper
2 tablespoons salad oil
½ cup chopped salami
1½ pounds ground chuck or round steak
1 tablespoon Worcestershire
1 cup catsup
1 teaspoon monosodium glutamate
Pinch of sweet basil or oregano
Pinch of thyme
8 ounces grated sharp Cheddar cheese

Cut loaf of bread in half and remove most of inside in small pieces picked out with the fingers. Sauté vegetables in oil until soft. Add salami, pieces of bread, and ground meat. Brown, stirring well to mix with vegetables. Add all remaining ingredients except cheese. Stir and turn until all is well mixed and beef is done. Stuff contents into French bread shells and spread cheese on top. Place in hot oven or under broiler until cheese melts, making sure crust does not burn.

This will feed two famished men; or if you wish to cut the halves again, it should easily take care of four ordinary grazers.

No-Name Pork Sandwiches

A late snack need not be elegant, but it should be good and substantial. Try this sandwich submitted by C. O. Ritter and see if it doesn't fill your bill. The timing is excellent because you can start it in the morning. Says he:

"The beauty of this recipe is that when the meat is placed in the oven, it can be forgotten until ready to serve. It is ideal for those late poker or bridge games, and it is also think-free for after-party serving.

"I must impress the importance of two items in its preparation: first, the defatting; and second, the foil seal, which must be as tight as possible."

5 pounds fresh pork leg or Boston butt, very lean
2 teaspoons salt
1 teaspoon seasoned pepper
About ¾ teaspoon liquid smoke
1 large onion, sliced
Hamburger buns, English muffins, or
sliced French bread
Sweet relish or barbecue sauce

Have your meatman bone the pork when you purchase it. Then it will be necessary for you to completely de-fat the meat prior to further preparation. All of the cover fat must be removed and discarded; in addition, any pockets or seams containing fat should also be trimmed out. The smallest possible amount of fat is the key to the success of this recipe.

Cut the remaining meat into small pieces (about 1 by 1 by 2 inches). You should have about 8 cups of pork cubes. In the bottom of a 9 by 5-inch loaf pan, place a layer of about ⅓ of the pork. Generously season with part of the salt, seasoned pepper, and ¼ teaspoon of liquid smoke (use with care, being careful not to overpower the delicate pork flavor with too much smoke). Place two slices of onion on this.

Continue adding two more layers, seasoning each as you did the first one, using all the remaining pork and seasonings.

Completely seal the loaf pan with three layers of heavy foil, going entirely around the pan with each wrapping and paying particular attention to crimping around the top. Place in a moderately slow oven (250°) for 10 hours.

After removing from oven, just prior to serving, take off foil and use two forks to shred meat completely while still in the pan. This will permit the meat to absorb most of the liquid meat juices.

Serve on toasted hamburger buns, English muffins, or French bread with sweet relish or your favorite barbecue sauce. Makes 10 to 12 servings.

⚛ King Oscar ⚛

Here is a remarkably agreeable combination of rye bread, sardines, and Mozarella or pizza cheese.

"I often experiment with light suppers," says Ted L. Cooper. "I concocted the following one evening from items I had on hand. It's a household snack specialty now."

Russian rye bread (2 slices per customer)
Mayonnaise
Mayonnaise-base dressing (specially seasoned for meat, fish, and cheese dishes)
Sardines
Mozarella cheese, sliced

Spread each slice of bread lightly with mayonnaise and mayonnaise-base dressing. Top with sardines and cheese slices. Oven-broil (about 2½ inches below flame or heating element) until cheese bubbles and browns slightly. Serve at once.

⚛ Tacos de Aguacate ⚛

"This dish is a specialty of our family," says Monte Millard, as he offers *Tacos de Aguacate* (avocado). Tacos, the Mexican equivalents of our sandwiches, are often served as a side dish, but they can be main dishes, too.

½ cup olive oil
4 cloves garlic
2 large Spanish onions, finely chopped
1 can (1 lb., 12 oz.) solid pack tomatoes
1 can (4 oz.) peeled green peppers, finely chopped
2 cans (8 oz. each) tomato sauce
Salt, pepper, and oregano
1 teaspoon sugar
Bacon fat or lard
1 dozen corn tortillas
Tillamook cheese
2 medium-sized avocados
Sour cream

In a deep saucepan, heat olive oil and add garlic. Remove garlic when golden brown, and discard. Add finely chopped onions and cook until golden brown. Add tomatoes, green peppers, and tomato sauce. Season to taste with salt, coarse black pepper, and oregano. Add sugar. Cover and simmer 45 minutes.

Heat bacon fat or lard in separate frying pan. Fry tortillas one at a time, first on one side and then the other, leaving them still quite flexible. Across the entire diameter of each tortilla, place a sliver of Tillamook and a sliver of avocado, wrap the tortilla into a roll, and secure with a toothpick. Arrange tacos in baking dish and pour over sauce from other pan. Heat in moderate oven (350°) for 25 minutes. Top with sour cream and serve 2 to a customer. Makes 6 tasty servings.

ℳ Blintzen con Queso ℳ

This recipe combines, of all things, Jewish with Mexican cookery in one of the happiest relationships you'll see in a long time. A piquant green chile and some soft white cheese lurk within an innocent looking blintz, so post warnings for guests with sensitive tongues.

Frank B. Julian, creator of the dish, explains it thus: "Cheese blintzes and flour tortilla quesadillas are favorites in my family, so I produced this successful hybrid combining their virtues.

"The result I have tentatively named Blintzen con Queso, but I will cheerfully defer to anyone who comes up with a better name."

BLINTZES

7 eggs
⅓ cup unsifted regular all-purpose flour
½ teaspoon salt
1½ cups milk
⅓ cup salad oil

FILLING

½ pound shredded jack cheese
1 can (4 oz.) California green chiles, seeded and cut in thin strips

To make blintzes, beat the eggs until frothy, beat in flour and salt, then the milk and salad oil. Heat a griddle over moderately low heat (about 325° on electric grill) and grease lightly. Pour on ¼ cup batter and tilt the griddle so that batter spreads evenly to about 6 inches in diameter.

When top looks dry, sprinkle about 2 tablespoons cheese on one half with several strips of chile; fold and cook for about 30 seconds longer.

Serve immediately, or hold in a warm oven while you cook the rest of batter.

Makes about 16 blintzes.

ℳ Yankee Pizza ℳ

For a hot lunch sandwich or a late evening snack, you might try what Art Hilts calls Yankee Pizza. It will never replace real Italian pizza, but was never intended to. It is simply a well seasoned combination of bacon, green onion, and cheese on a bun—and don't sneer before tasting. It may appeal to you even more than to your teen-age children, should you be blessed with any.

6 slices bacon, diced
5 or 6 green onions, sliced fine
½ pound American cheese, mild or medium sharp
1 teaspoon monosodium glutamate
¼ teaspoon salt
A few grindings of coarse black pepper
Dash of cayenne
½ cup mayonnaise
6 hamburger buns, split

Scramble bacon in frying pan over medium heat until it curls. Add green onions and cook until limp. Remove from heat and drain off at least half the bacon drippings. Coarsely shred cheese into a bowl. Stir cheese into bacon-onion mixture along with monosodium glutamate, salt, pepper, cayenne, and mayonnaise. Spread on split hamburger buns; place under broiler and toast until brown. Makes 6 servings.

California Coffee Cake

No breakfast guest would go away disappointed if you served very tender coffee cake made according to the recipe of John R. Reynolds. It is relatively simple to make and could easily become a Sunday morning household favorite—in either variation.

FILLING
½ cup brown sugar, packed
1 teaspoon cinnamon
1 tablespoon butter, melted
1 tablespoon flour
½ cup chopped walnuts

BATTER
½ cup butter or shortening
1 cup sugar
2 eggs, separated
1½ cups flour
1 teaspoon salt
2 teaspoons baking powder
Grated peel of 1 small to medium-sized lemon
Grated peel of 1 medium-sized to large orange
½ cup milk

Mix together the filling ingredients, mashing all lumps out of sugar, and set aside.

Cream butter or shortening and gradually work in sugar. Add yolks of the 2 eggs and beat well. Sift flour, measure, and sift with salt and baking powder; mix in. Add orange and lemon peel and beat batter rapidly for a few seconds; stir in milk. Beat egg whites until stiff but not dry, and fold into batter.

Pour about four-fifths of the batter into a well greased 9-inch-square baking pan and smooth it evenly over the bottom of pan. Sprinkle filling lightly over batter, then drizzle remaining batter over the filling. It is not necessary to cover the filling; any that shows through will give a nice mottled effect.

Bake in moderate oven (350°) for 40 to 45 min-utes, or until nicely browned. Run cake knife around inside edges of pan, then shake or knock cake loose. Cool on wire rack. Cut into pieces, and serve warm or cool. You can wrap in foil and store in the refrigerator. Makes about 9 generous pieces.

Superb Variation

Use black walnuts in place of English walnuts in filling; eliminate orange and lemon peel from batter. Instead, mash 1 large or 2 small ripe bananas (or liquefy in blender) and add to blended shortening-sugar-egg yolk mixture along with the dry ingredients. Reduce milk to ⅓ cup. (It will be a little thicker or stiffer than the batter without bananas.) Then fold in beaten egg whites and proceed as prescribed above.

⚡ Cornmeal Mountain Pancakes ⚡

Forest ranger Dick Zediker sings the praises of his recipe as follows: "I hereby submit these cornmeal pancakes, made many times here in my cabin. The recipe came to me from an old mountaineer and miner, beard and all, who lives in a log cabin in the high country. Please note the flavor, the texture, and how nicely they brown. Served with a skillet full of fresh-caught trout and plenty of strong coffee—what more could a man ask for?"

Anybody who's tasted these will go along with Dick. Unless you hate cornmeal, these are good, hearty, light pancakes. Make plenty.

Dick also suggests using home-soured milk instead of buttermilk. Mix 4 teaspoons of lemon juice or vinegar into 1¼ cups regular milk and let stand 5 minutes.

1 egg
1¼ cups buttermilk or home-soured milk
1 tablespoon molasses
¼ cup melted shortening
1 cup unsifted all-purpose flour
1 teaspoon salt
½ teaspoon soda
2 teaspoons baking powder
½ cup yellow cornmeal

Beat together the egg, milk, molasses, and shortening. Add the flour, sifted with the salt, soda, and baking powder; also add cornmeal, and stir just until well blended. Bake on a moderately hot greased griddle. Makes about 16 pancakes, 4 inches in diameter.

⚡ Eggnog Waffles ⚡

Curtis Y. Joe presents his fine formula for Eggnog Waffles. You'll be surprised how much you taste the eggnog in these waffles; it seems just as appropriate there as in the traditional drink. Another very nice touch is the walnuts. Actually, you could substitute any other kind of nuts you might have around the house (no offense intended).

⅔ cup buttermilk
⅓ cup commercial eggnog
1 egg, slightly beaten
1 tablespoon salad oil
¼ teaspoon soda
Dash of nutmeg
1 cup prepared pancake mix
¼ cup chopped walnuts

Mix together the buttermilk, eggnog, egg, oil, soda, and nutmeg. Then add the pancake mix and chopped walnuts and mix again. (If desired, the egg can be separated, and the white beaten and folded in last.) Bake in hot waffle iron. Makes 2 to 4 servings, depending on appetite.

⚛ **Orange-Raisin Bread** ⚛

No one can resist shouting encouragement when he spies a man rowing upstream. Not that you expect him to make much headway by such apparent refutation of logic. But he does develop muscle, and he certainly proves that going with the current isn't always inevitable.

A worthy upstream-rower is Robert E. Goldsworthy who introduces his recipe for Orange-Raisin Bread with a directive "First make some candied orange peel."

"Of course," he admits, "in this day of the bake-in-the-box prepared mix, one may question the common sense of making orange peel at home. However, the home-candied peel is what gives this bread its distinctive character. Use commercial candied peel only when it cannot be avoided."

1 package yeast, active dry or compressed
2 cups warm (lukewarm for compressed yeast) water
About 6 cups unsifted all-purpose flour
1 tablespoon salt
2 egg yolks
¼ cup melted shortening
2 cups golden raisins
1 cup candied orange peel (recipe follows)

The night before you intend to bake, dissolve yeast in 1 cup warm water. Stir into 2 cups flour, into which the salt has been mixed. Set aside in covered bowl.

The next day, whip egg yolks with melted shortening. Add ¼ cup warm water and whip like mad to emulsify the shortening and water. Add this to the dough mixture that was set aside overnight and stir well. Add ¾ cup warm water and about 4 cups flour and knead on floured board for 10 minutes. Toward the end of the kneading, incorporate the raisins and candied orange peel.

Place dough in a well greased bowl, cover, and place in warm place until doubled in bulk. Punch down and divide dough in half. Roll out each half on a floured board with rolling pin to make a sheet about ½ inch thick and as wide as a loaf pan is long. Roll each half up like a jelly roll, pinching the dough together to keep it from unrolling. Place in greased loaf pans (9 by 5-inch size) with the pinched seams toward the bottom. Let rise until top of each loaf is about ¾ inch above top of pan.

Bake in hot oven (400°) for 30 to 35 minutes. Remove from oven and immediately turn out of pans to cool on wire racks. When cooled, slice fairly thick and pop into toaster or serve as is—with plenty of butter. Makes 2 loaves.

If a loaf should escape almost instant destruction, it makes marvelous French toast when one day old.

Candied Orange Peel

Peel a minimum of 6 large navel oranges by slitting the rind in quarters and carefully removing it in uniform pieces. With a sharp knife and a cutting board, dice the rind into cubes about ¼ inch on a side. Measure the diced peel and empty into a frying pan with cover. Add an equal volume of sugar to the pan. Stir well and place over low heat. The sugar will draw moisture from the peel, making a syrup in which to cook it. Keep stirring as the heat is increased.

When the syrup begins to boil, cover and cook gently until the cubes become translucent, about 15 minutes. Then remove the cover and continue to boil, stirring from time to time, until the syrup is almost evaporated, 10 or 15 minutes longer. Spoon the mass onto a cooky sheet and let stand for a couple of days. When cubes are dry, break into separate units, store in a jar with a tight lid, adding ¼ cup brandy to each 2 cups of peel. So treated, the peel will keep for months during that distressing period when navels are not available.

⚛ Blintzes with Corners ⚛

Orron Qualls offers his version of the blintz. The blintz "wrapping" is usually round, just like a pancake, but Orron has an individual method which you may consider optional: "I use the electric pan and use only part of it, so the cake ends up in a rectangular shape—about 6 by 10 inches."

5 eggs
1 cup milk
½ teaspoon salt
¾ cup flour
About ¼ cup (½ cube) butter

FILLING

½ cup diced ham
1 medium-sized onion, diced
8 sprigs parsley, finely chopped
Finely chopped chives
Herbs of your choice
½ cup diced green peppers
½ cup (1 cube) butter
2 cups chopped mushrooms
½ cup red wine
1 cup cheese sauce, either canned or homemade

Beat eggs, milk, and salt together. Stir in flour until well mixed. Melt butter in a frying pan or electric frying pan, pour in batter enough for a good-sized individual cake, and fry on both sides. Repeat until all batter is used up. Set blintzes aside.

For the filling, combine ham, onion, parsley, chives (and other herbs), and green peppers in a frying pan and sauté in butter. When vegetables are partly cooked, add mushrooms and wine. Continue cooking until mixture has thickened a little.

Roll filling in blintzes and place in baking dish. Pour cheese sauce over blintzes and place under broiler until cheese browns. As an added fancy touch, if you wish, add a tablespoon of brandy and flame the dish before bringing it to the table. Makes 6 blintzes, measuring about 6 to 10 inches.

APPETIZING APPETIZERS

If you'd like to know how much a man really cares about how food tastes and how it is presented, observe what he serves to nibble with cocktails. It is perhaps a brutal test to impose, but it is truth-revealing.

The very simple things that require none of the skills of a card-carrying chef do very nicely for many occasions. But the recipes presented in this chapter are good to keep in mind when you want to add one or two more dramatic specialties to the selection. Variety is the secret. The quantities need not be large to make an impression. When these foods are just the preamble to a meal soon to follow, they shouldn't be too hearty.

On the other side of the coin—or the appetizer tray—there are several tidbits that can be boldly and fearlessly put together in proportions and quantities that make them a very pleasant end unto themselves.

In this chapter you will find a very few dips, some barbecued and some deep-fried things, mushrooms and other vegetables, shrimp, oysters, caviar, and others more difficult to classify. The Post-Poker Platter is perhaps more of a snack than an appetizer, but the difference is minor; a good many of these would go well for a midnight supper.

➳ Rock Salt Oysters ⟋⟍

"People who like oysters, but hesitate to tackle them in the shell, shouldn't shy away from this recipe," reports William L. Johnson, Sr. "I often buy shucked oysters in the fish markets, and use oyster shells that are left over from previous occasions."

If you suffer a dearth of oyster shells, try scallop shells instead. You can buy these in specialty food stores and import shops if you have trouble finding real oyster shells.

Although Bill refers to this as an appetizer, six or eight on a plate with some salad and crusty bread would make a very fine lunch or dinner.

1 dozen oysters in the shell (or 1 dozen
shucked oysters and 12 half shells)
Rock salt
1 cup cracker crumbs
¾ cup Chablis
Monosodium glutamate
About 4 tablespoons butter
¼ cup grated Parmesan cheese

Scrub oyster shells with vegetable brush under cold, running water before opening, or have them opened at the fish market. Remove from shell and drain in colander 10 to 15 minutes. Fill a large baking pan 1 inch deep with rock salt, and arrange oyster or scallop shells on it. Roll the oysters in cracker crumbs, place one in each half shell, and add 1 tablespoon Chablis to each. Sprinkle each with dash monosodium glutamate, put about 1 teaspoon butter on top, then sprinkle on the Parmesan. Bake in a moderate oven (350°) for about 30 minutes. Makes 2 servings for a meal, up to 12 as an appetizer.

Serving suggestion: Fill individual wooden salad bowls with rock salt, and serve the oysters in these.

➳ Happy Hour Mushrooms ⟋⟍

"An effort to enjoy mushrooms in a little different way than the traditional ones worked out quite well for me," says Clifton W. Royston. "Don't let the name fool you; they won't last more than 10 minutes."

½ pound small to medium-sized mushrooms
About 2 tablespoons melted butter
4 tablespoons soft butter
1 small clove garlic, minced or mashed
3 tablespoons finely diced or shredded jack cheese
2 tablespoons red wine
1 teaspoon soy sauce
⅓ cup fine cracker crumbs

Remove stems from mushrooms and save for other cooking. Brush mushroom caps with the melted butter. Combine the soft butter with garlic; add cheese and mix in well. Add wine and soy sauce, then the cracker crumbs to make a paste. Fill the mushroom caps with this paste. Place on a foil-covered cooky sheet and put under a broiler about 5 inches from heat for about 3 minutes, or until bubbly and lightly browned. Serve with toothpicks and a few crackers, if desired. Makes about 16 appetizers.

❀ Succulent Subrics ❀

Have you ever noticed the distinguished dishes (Veal Scaloppini, Salmis) that are based on very thin, small, tender slices of meat? Here's another from a discriminating recipe sleuth, Bradley T. Scheer. This snack *par excellence* is fine for pre-dinner finger food, could go well for breakfast, or put it anywhere else you like.

3 eggs
¾ cup freshly shredded Swiss cheese
1 tablespoon flour
½ teaspoon salt
⅛ teaspoon pepper, or to taste
1 pound beef or veal round, sliced thin and cut in 1-inch squares
¼ cup butter or salad oil, or a mixture of the two

Beat eggs and mix with them the cheese, flour, salt, and pepper. Coat the squares of meat with the egg-cheese batter and fry in the butter or oil. Makes about 36 cheese-coated slices.

❀ Chicken Liver Piroshki ❀

Piroshki are little Russian pastries that are usually served with tea in the afternoon, but go just as well in the evening as hot hors d'oeuvres. The name translates as "little pies," but the filling is almost always meat or vegetables. A. A. Horton's version calls for chicken livers, enveloped by a buttery sour cream pastry that he has brought to full fruition.

PASTRY

1 cup regular all-purpose flour
⅛ teaspoon salt
½ cup (1 cube) butter
3 tablespoons commercial sour cream

FILLING

2 tablespoons butter
4 chicken livers
½ cup sliced mushrooms
½ teaspoon salt
⅛ teaspoon pepper

For the pastry, sift flour and measure; then sift with salt in a bowl. Add butter and cut in with pastry blender or work lightly with fingers until well blended. Add sour cream and mix until smooth. Wrap in waxed paper and chill 2 hours or overnight. To prepare filling, melt butter in a small frying pan. Add livers, mushrooms, salt, and pepper, and cook over low heat about 6 minutes. Turn out on a board and chop fine; set aside. To assemble, roll pastry ⅛ inch thick on lightly floured board. Cut rounds 2 inches in diameter. On each, place a rounded teaspoonful of filling; fold over pastry, moisten edges, and seal carefully. Arrange on an ungreased baking sheet and bake in a hot oven (400°) for 20 minutes, or until golden brown.

❈ Shrimp Beau Brummell ❈

Bixele Bialiej offers a deceptively simple combination that looks decorative and tastes good. He calls it Shrimp Beau Brummell, after that polished Regency beau (so polished he even shined the soles of his shoes). The comparison is apt, since the dish is most elegant in appearance with its red halved shrimp, sliced mushrooms, and border of quartered yellow lemons.

Ideally, this dish should serve to introduce a meal, since it is too light to stand entirely alone.

8 large shrimp or prawns
6 large mushrooms
1 tablespoon olive oil
1 tablespoon butter
½ clove garlic
½ teaspoon oregano
¼ cup dry white wine (sauterne)
1 lemon, quartered

Clean shrimp and halve lengthwise. Slice mushrooms, and sauté in olive oil and butter to which garlic has been added. Add shrimp and oregano, sauté 5 minutes more, and add wine. Taste before salting. Serve in heated casserole bordered with lemon quarters. Makes about 2 servings.

❈ Earthy Mushrooms ❈

If you're a patsy for any dish that uses good mushrooms generously, try these hors d'oeuvres devised by Dr. Jack H. Silveira. The introduction of the mushroom stems provides the meat mixture the right touch of earthy flavor to match that of the mushroom caps. The caps, by the way, need be only large enough to hold the meat, in case you prefer your mushrooms fairly small.

16 large mushrooms (about 2 inches in diameter)
½ cup soy sauce
½ pound lean ground beef
¼ cup minced green peppers
2 tablespoons fine dry bread crumbs
1 egg yolk
1 tablespoon minced onion
½ clove garlic, crushed
¼ teaspoon salt
¼ teaspoon pepper

Remove stems from mushrooms and scoop out a little of the flesh to form a depression inside each mushroom cap. Save stems and pieces; marinate caps in soy for about 1 hour. If soy does not cover them, turn them occasionally.

Finely chop mushroom stems and pieces and mix with all remaining ingredients. Remove mushroom caps from soy; drain and fill with meat mixture, mounding up the surface. Brush meat with soy. Broil in the oven until meat and mushrooms are done to your liking, 8 to 10 minutes, basting frequently with the soy. If you have to hold them for any length of time, they can be reheated in a moderate oven (350°). Serve hot to eat with a fork as a first course at table; or, if mushrooms are small enough, serve as finger food. Serve at least 2 mushrooms per guest.

⚞ Pobrecito ⚟

The foodstuffs employed in Mexican cookery seem remarkably compatible and can be combined more freely and directly with one another than the foodstuffs of almost any other land. (To strum quickly over the list . . . *tortilla, chile, frijole, tomate, queso, carne, cebolla, pescado.*) Consequently, you can cook in Mexican style with a very free hand, as does Phimister B. Proctor in the improvisation that follows.

He queries, "This could be called a Mexican pizza?" It also somewhat resembles a dish called *Tostados*, and still another called *Chalupas*. The name *Pobrecito* is a very rough translation of Poor Boy (sandwich); the two are much alike in spirit.

1 tortilla
Butter or bacon fat
Chopped canned green chiles
Refried beans
Chopped onion
Shredded sharp Cheddar cheese

TOPPINGS

Small bits of chorizo (Mexican sausage),
cooked meat, or cooked chicken
Anchovies, shrimp, or crab
Pickled mushrooms
Small strips of pimiento or green pepper
Small slivers of tomato
Toasted pumpkin seeds

Fry the tortilla in the butter or bacon fat until browned slightly, but still limp. Remove to a warmed plate. Spread or sprinkle on top layers of the following in the order given: chiles, beans, onion, and cheese. Dot the surface of the cheese layer (the top one) with any one ingredient from the above list of toppings. Or create your own topping with a Mexican flavor.

Place under broiler until cheese is melted. Remove and cut into strips and serve as hors d'oeuvres, as a side dish, or as a main dish. Serve with salsa or chile sauce.

⚞ Caviar Pie ⚟

When you're entertaining in fine style, bring on Dr. George Selleck's Caviar Pie. It need not be served in quantity to win high praise from your guests.

1 pint commercial sour cream
Juice of 1 small lemon
7-inch baked pastry shell
2 tablespoons chopped chives
8 ounces caviar

Place sour cream in a cloth and hang up to drain overnight. Add lemon juice to sour cream and spread into pie shell. Sprinkle with chopped chives. Carefully spread caviar over the top.

Cut into small wedges to serve.

⚡ Gizzard Delights ⚡

"Growing up years ago in an area where we ate chicken when we could not afford meat, I learned that the best part of the chicken is the gizzard. It disturbs me that gizzards are nowadays so lowly rated, as judged by comparative prices in the market. This disturbance led me into some experimental cooking, which may be of interest," relates Howard E. Wilson.

"Chicken gizzards make an ideal hot addition to hors d'oeuvres at cocktail time," he continues, "and they are not at all hard to prepare. Buy about two pounds of medium-sized gizzards in the market. Cut out the gristle sections (a job not nearly as difficult as deveining shrimp or wrapping slices of bacon around pieces of liver), leaving two or three pieces from each gizzard, which can be cooked many ways.

"One is simply to roll them in flour with salt and pepper and fry in reasonably deep fat. This will please older chicken fanciers. Another way is to marinate the gizzards in white wine, red wine, or soy sauce with appropriate spices. After considerable experimentation, the recipe I like best is as follows."

> 2 pounds chicken gizzards
> 1½ cups dry white wine
> 1 bay leaf
> ½ teaspoon celery seed
> ½ teaspoon dill weed
> ¼ teaspoon oregano
> ¼ teaspoon rosemary
> ¼ teaspoon thyme
> ⅛ teaspoon black pepper
> ½ cup regular all-purpose flour
> 1 teaspoon salt
> Cooking oil

Prepare gizzards by removing gristle and cutting into bite-sized chunks. Marinate for about 1½ hours in a mixture of wine, bay leaf, celery seed, dill weed, oregano, rosemary, thyme, and black pepper. Remove from marinade; shake in a plastic or paper bag containing flour and salt. Fry in hot fat (375°) until they are crisp and brown, about 2 minutes. Serve hot with individual wooden picks. Makes about 80 to 90 bite-sized morsels.

It is difficult to prepare an oversupply for cocktail guests, particularly if you do not tell them what they are eating until they have tasted it.

✺ Flower Fritters ✺

This unusual fritter is made by dipping flowers of zucchini in batter, then deep-fat frying. Of course, there is only an outside chance you may have zucchini in flower in your home garden, but Dr. George Selleck's delicacy is worth trying whenever you can get the ingredients. (The Coachella, Imperial, and San Diego areas of Southern California grow zucchini right through the winter. Some markets specializing in Italian foods sell zucchini flowers through the summer in bunches of a dozen or so—about 30 cents a bunch in San Francisco.)

2 eggs, separated
⅔ cup milk
1 tablespoon olive oil
1 tablespoon lemon juice
½ teaspoon salt
⅔ cup flour
2 tablespoons sautéed onion
2 tablespoons Parmesan cheese
2 tablespoons Bourbon whiskey
About 2 dozen large zucchini blossoms
Flour
Salad oil

Whip egg yolks until lemon colored. Add milk, olive oil, lemon juice, salt, and ⅔ cup sifted flour. Purée the onion and add with the Parmesan cheese and whiskey. Set batter aside for an hour or more. Just before using, fold in the whites of egg which have been whipped, but not to the point of dryness.

Wash flowers of zucchini and drain well (best handled by shaking each flower and placing on a piece of absorbent paper). Dust flour on a few at a time or place flour in a bag and toss a few at a time. Arrange on a piece of waxed paper, dip into batter, and deep fry in salad oil at 350° to 375°. Keep turning until flowers are golden brown. Arrange on a napkin and serve immediately.

✺ Post-Poker Platter ✺

To give this dish its due, don't feel that it must be reserved for poker parties. Any time the occasion—male, female, or mixed—calls for hearty sandwiches served direct from the kitchen, here are excellent candidates. John Strang's simple method of preparation rates even higher praise.

Before the other players come, prepare the following open-faced sandwiches, cover with foil or clear plastic film, and chill until 20 minutes or so before you want to eat. Use either buffet rye or any dark, very thinly sliced bread.

For sandwich type I, cover each buttered bread slice with a very thin slice of tomato and two small sardines, and very generously sprinkle with grated Parmesan cheese.

For type II, put a thin slice of cheese (sharp Tillamook is especially good here) on the bread, and top with a couple of drained smoked oysters.

For type III, spread shredded Swiss cheese on lightly buttered bread; top with slices or flakes of smoked fish of your choice.

Slide the sandwich platter under the broiler and broil until hot and the cheese is slightly bubbly. Serve these with crisp celery sticks, green onions, radishes, and sliced white radishes, along with plenty of dark beer or ale.

⚓ Sprouts and Double-T Sauce ⚓

Those who consider the Brussels sprout a rather dull vegetable may do a double take if they ever encounter it with Double-T Sauce—a "terrific tartar" sauce devised and christened by Mort Greene. If you have capers around the house, you may be happy to find here another way to use them.

Pick out small Brussels sprouts if you intend to serve them on toothpicks. One dip in the sauce and they lose that "cole crop taste," as one garden-minded taster put it.

2 pounds Brussels sprouts

SAUCE

1½ cups mayonnaise
4 tablespoons sweet pickle relish
4 tablespoons capers and juice
1 teaspoon sugar
1 tablespoon grated onion
Salt to taste
Pepper to taste
Dash of cayenne
Vinegar (to thin slightly)

Cook sprouts in about 1 inch of boiling salted water until barely done, not soggy. Chill. Combine all sauce ingredients: skewer each sprout on a toothpick and serve with a bowl of the sauce to be used as a dip. Or toss sprouts with sauce and serve as salad at a buffet. Makes about 30 medium-sized appetizers.

⚓ Tangy Sardine Dip ⚓

What for hors d'oeuvres? is always a moot question. Here's a stout answer, strong on fish flavor. If one can of sardines is too much, you could cut back to as little as half a can. Ralph D. Lee suggests serving with barbecue chips (smoky in flavor), but the dip is equally good or better on some vehicle with less pronounced flavor of its own. Plain potato chips, little crackers, and thin slices of rye bread are good.

2 cloves garlic, pressed
1 large package (8 oz.) cream cheese
1 can (3¾ oz.) Norwegian sardines, drained and mashed
⅛ teaspoon powdered beef stock base
Salt and pepper to taste
3 tablespoons sauterne

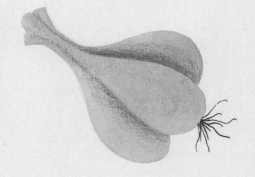

Thoroughly mix all ingredients. Serve on crackers or chips of your choice. Makes about 2 cups dip.

❧ Spicy Meatball Appetizers ❧

"This is a wonderful hot appetizer kept warm in a chafing dish or casserole, served with toothpicks and crackers or any chip-type favorite," says Jules Greenberg. "Children as well as adults really go for this dish; it makes the party."

With no more ado than a passing comment that curry lovers might like to add more curry, here for you to savor are Spicy Meatball Appetizers.

1 onion, finely chopped
1 cup fine dry bread crumbs
2 pounds ground round or sirloin
3 eggs
½ teaspoon salt
¼ teaspoon pepper
½ teaspoon seasoning salt
¾ teaspoon curry powder, or to taste
¼ cup grated Parmesan cheese
½ teaspoon Worcestershire
2 cloves garlic
1 cup flour
Salad oil or shortening
1 cup red wine
½ cup beef consommé
2 small cans (8 oz. each) tomato sauce
⅛ to ¼ teaspoon oregano (optional, but good)

Add onion and bread crumbs to meat, mix thoroughly, then add the eggs and mix again. Add salt, pepper, seasoning salt, curry, Parmesan cheese and Worcestershire and again mix well by hand until blended in. Crush one clove of garlic and mix it in.

Roll meat into small balls about 1½ inches in diameter; roll lightly in flour. Crush other clove of garlic and add to oil in large frying pan. Fill pan with as many meatballs as it will take; cook, turning with a fork, about 8 minutes, or until well browned.

Meanwhile combine wine, consommé, tomato sauce, and oregano in a large saucepan and simmer while the first meatballs are frying. As meatballs are done, add to sauce and continue to simmer all for about 25 to 35 minutes. Add meatballs and sauce to chafing dish, serve with large toothpicks, and they will disappear at once.

If sauce needs more liquid, add some more of the beef consommé.

Makes about 80 small meatballs.

✖ Succulent Cheese Balls ✖

Before you sit your guests down to dinner, pass a platter of Dr. George Selleck's Succulent Cheese Balls, along with glasses of champagne, if the budget is willing. George suggests three variations on the major cooking scheme, should you wish to experiment, or find the first cooking method unsuited to your needs.

1 cup milk
½ cup (1 cube) butter
1 cup sifted flour
3 eggs
2 ounces Gruyère cheese cut into small cubes
2 ounces diced lean ham
⅓ cup slivered almonds

Heat milk and butter in saucepan until butter is melted; add sifted flour. Cook and stir batter until it leaves sides of pan and forms a ball. Beat in eggs, one at a time. Fold in cheese, ham, almonds.

Form the paste into balls the size of a small lime and arrange 2 inches apart on a greased cooky sheet.

Bake 15 minutes in a hot oven (425°); reduce oven heat to 325° and bake 10 to 15 minutes longer, or until done. Makes 2 dozen. Serve as finger food.

Variations: (1) Roll on a floured board and deep fry. (2) Bake in a 9-inch cakepan. (3) Form into a ring and bake on a greased cooky sheet.

✖ Wine Mushroom Appeteasers ✖

The only point of conflict in Colonel E. Jeff Barnette's recipe may be the size of the mushrooms: you may wish them larger or smaller.

1 pound medium-sized mushrooms
½ cup (1 cube) butter or margarine
½ teaspoon monosodium glutamate
1 tablespoon minced green onions
1 tablespoon minced parsley
1 small clove garlic, crushed
1 cup dry white wine
Salt and pepper to taste

Clean mushrooms; remove stems and save for use some other time in soup. Place butter in heavy frying pan. Sprinkle mushrooms with monosodium glutamate and sauté in butter for 5 minutes. Add onion, parsley, garlic, wine, salt, and pepper. Sauté a few minutes longer until mushrooms are done. Serve on toothpicks as appetizers, or serve as an accompaniment to any meat dish. Makes 6 servings as a dinner side dish.

✒ Roquefort-Cognac Crisps ✒

A. E. Clamp has just the kind of hors d'oeuvre or all purpose snack that many a man is seeking—the bite-in-hand with enough substance to be nourishing. It is not too goopy, and you don't have to set up a regular conveyor belt of crackers or chips in order to get the really choice stuff into your mouth.

If you'd like apple slices that lie flat, cut each cored apple in half lengthwise, lay each half on its cut side, and slice it crosswise.

3 ounces Roquefort cheese
2 tablespoons butter
2 tablespoons brandy
3 red apples
Lemon juice

Mix cheese, butter, and brandy; cover and keep in refrigerator overnight or longer. Core apples, but leave unpeeled. Cut into ½-inch slices and dip quickly in lemon juice to prevent darkening. Spread with cheese-butter-brandy mixture and serve, with crackers on the side for those who want them.

✒ Oysters Parmesan ✒

Captain W. B. Moore, USN, says, "After several years of duty in the tropics, we certainly enjoyed being back on the Pacific Coast where there was such an abundance of superlative seafood, and this recipe was one result of our exultation."

It completely lives up to his description:"A flashy, tasty, and unique hors d'oeuvre— a sure fire conversation piece whether your guests like oysters or not."

EQUIPMENT	INGREDIENTS
10 to 12 oyster shells, other suitable concave shells, or improvised shells of heavy foil, to hold oysters and sauce	1 pint medium-sized oysters, fresh or frozen
Rock salt	4 tablespoons butter
Bottom portion of a beer can, about 1½ inches tall, or equivalent	2 tablespoons chopped fresh parsley
Ethyl alcohol, for flaming	2 tablespoons chopped green onions
	4 tablespoons grated Parmesan cheese
	4 tablespoons cracker crumbs
	Salt and Pepper to taste

Dry oysters carefully on paper toweling. While they're on paper, cut into bite-sized pieces—usually in thirds. Arrange each cut-up oyster in an oyster shell. With a fork, mash together the butter, parsley, and green onions. Put about ½ teaspoon of this mixture on each oyster. Mix cheese and cracker crumbs and add salt and pepper to taste; then put about a heaping teaspoon on each oyster.

Fill a large, rectangular, ovenproof glass baking dish with about 1½ inches of rock salt. Bury the cut-off can, open side up, so the rim is barely visible at the salt level. Fill the can with salt, too. Nestle the oyster shells close together in rock salt, but not over the buried can.

Bake in 425° oven for 20 to 25 minutes, until oysters bubble and the tops brown. Remove from the oven, carefully pour some alcohol into the can, light, and serve the dish ablaze, with toothpicks and lemon wedges adjacent. The salt, of course, conducts heat and takes the place of a chafing dish. (Watch out for the heat on a finished table top; use lots of insulation or elevate the glass dish.) Makes 10 to 12 servings.

❦ Lime-"Cooked" Fish ❦

"The natives of many South Pacific islands eat a quantity of what they call 'raw fish,'" tells Robert Ferris, "but their designation is a misnomer, because they soak the fish in lime juice for an hour or more in the course of preparation and the citric acid in the lime juice brings about chemically many of the changes that occur in cooking with heat. The fish loses its transparency and the characteristic smell of raw fish and takes on the more opaque appearance of heat-cooked fish."

(The fact that you find something very similar, called *Ceviche*, in certain Latin American countries would seem to bolster Thor Heyerdahl's *Kon-Tiki* theory of an early sea route between South America and the South Pacific.)

When you serve this to guests, some may try it quite cautiously the first time. One was heard to comment, "Interesting, and proves it can be done—but is it enjoyable?" Most of the others, however, will be wholeheartedly favorable, stipulating only their preference that the fish be a notably firm and fine-textured one.

> 1 pound bonito or similar firm, white ocean fish (skinned and boned)
> 1 large onion (half of it thinly sliced in rounds, the rest finely chopped)
> ½ pint fresh or reconstituted lime juice (not sweetened)
> Lettuce
> Sliced tomatoes
> Salt and pepper to taste

Cut the fish into thin slices about ¼ inch thick and place a layer of them in the bottom of a deep dish, such as a large soup plate. Sprinkle a little finely chopped onion on the layer of fish, then saturate it with lime juice. Repeat with additional layers until all the fish and chopped onion are used, but reserve a little of the lime juice. Place the fish in the refrigerator for 2 or 3 hours. Then drain, rinse with a little water, and drain again, thoroughly.

Serve on a bed of lettuce with tomato slices and thin-sliced rounds of onion. Sprinkle with a little fresh lime juice and season to taste with salt and pepper. Served in this manner, the raw fish makes an excellent salad of 4 to 6 servings.

Without the tomato and lettuce, it is a very satis-factory hors d'oeuvre. The Tahitians would insist that it must be served with coconut cream to be used either as a sauce or a dip. The coconut cream is made by grating the meat of a fresh coconut (averages about 3 cups) into ¼ to ½ cup of milk previously drained from the nut (on the mainland you might use cow's milk to fill out the liquid). This mixture is brought to a boil and simmered gently a few minutes.

After the mixture has cooled, separate the grated coconut from the milk by pouring the mixture through a piece of clean cheesecloth. Then wring out the cloth and its contents very firmly, until all of the creamy material in the grated coconut is expressed and added to the milk. When the mixture is chilled, it is ready to use as sauce or dressing for raw fish.

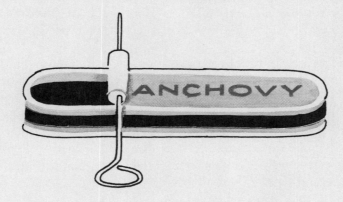

SOUPS AND STEWS

Soup, stews, and casseroles all are mixtures of foods. They range from wet—or soupy—to relatively dry, as are some of the casserole dishes. In fact, a few of the recipes in this chapter can be manipulated in either a wet or dry direction. One classifies as "a fairly dry soup or a fairly wet casserole." Another is frankly labeled a "souce" because it can serve either as a hearty soup or as a rich sauce to serve over rice.

Although none are termed "souperole" or "stoup," several could fit into such coined categories. A lot depends on just how much water you use—today's stew could be tomorrow's soup.

As a group, the recipes in this chapter are more original, personalized, individual, custom-made than any others in the book. In some aspects of their cooking, men are more inclined to bow—or at least nod—toward tradition; but with soups, stews, and casseroles they feel perfectly free to move entirely in directions of their own choosing.

A cook can either take a classic or well known recipe and adapt his needs to it, or he can reverse course and shape the recipe until it conforms to his needs, desires, or even whims. The contributors of the recipes in this chapter definitely took the latter course; there's an individual story behind practically every one.

French Onion Casserole

Herman Wiegmink introduces this recipe with the following explanation: "We love French Onion Soup, but somehow, seldom find the right occasions for soup. So we came up with French Onion Casserole."

Call it a fairly dry soup, or a fairly wet casserole; it makes a great accompaniment for plain meats. Some guides to quantities of the grated cheeses, have been specified, but you may want to play them by ear. Beware of browning the top too long under the broiler; the croutons then become almost impossibly chewy.

5 medium-sized onions, sliced
2 tablespoons butter
2 tablespoons flour
½ cup bouillon
¼ cup sherry
Salt to taste
Pepper to taste
1½ cups garlic-flavored croutons, mixed with 2 tablespoons melted butter
¾ cup shredded Swiss cheese
⅓ cup grated Parmesan cheese

Sauté onions in butter until they just start to turn golden colored. Sprinkle with flour, stir in bouillon; simmer 5 minutes. Add sherry, taste and add salt and pepper to taste. Top with buttered croutons, sprinkle with cheeses, and place under broiler just until cheese melts, about 2 minutes. Serve hot. Makes 4 servings.

Shrimp-Scallop "Souce"

Depending on your treatment of the following recipe, you'll end up with a hearty soup or a rich shrimp-scallop sauce to serve with rice. As John Ax points out, the best thing about it is its simplicity.

1 pound frozen scallops
Boiling salted water
2 cans (10 oz. each) shrimp soup, defrosted
1 can (6 or 8 oz.) sliced mushrooms, drained
Light cream (optional)
Cooked rice (optional)
1 to 2 cups cooked or canned shrimp, deveined and drained (optional)
Sherry to taste

Cook scallops in boiling salted water for 5 to 7 minutes, drain, and cut into small pieces. Heat soup in top of double boiler, and add scallops and mushrooms.

If you want to use this mixture for soup, stir in about 1½ cups light cream and about ½ cup rice, if you wish. Add sherry to taste. Reheat until hot. Serve from a tureen. Makes 6 servings.

To use it as a sauce, omit cream and add the cooked or canned shrimp, if you wish. Add sherry to taste. Serve over hot cooked rice. Makes about 6 servings.

❊ Salmon Soup ❊

First catch your salmon—many would say you get better odds if you try it in the Pacific Northwest.

And then? Listen to the words of Fred L. Delkin, Jr., speaking confidently from a vantage point in Portland:

"Struck one September by the terrible waste of feeding already fat seagulls the residue of a successful salmon fishing expedition, I concocted the following dish. It has since become a requested rite of each subsequent trip to the salmon grounds with my fishing companions.

"If you buy the fish, tell the man to leave head and tail attached. Finicky types can remove the eyes before cooking."

Salmon head, tail, fins, and backbone and
ribs if you fillet the raw fish
About 8 cups water
1 medium-sized onion, chopped
1 tablespoon butter
1 tablespoon olive oil
1 clove garlic, crushed
1 teaspoon dill weed
1½ teaspoons coriander seed
⅛ teaspoon cayenne pepper, or to taste
3 teaspoons salt, or to taste
Chopped fresh parsley

Put salmon parts into a large pot; add water (it should cover bones), onion, butter, olive oil, garlic, dill weed, coriander, pepper, and salt. Simmer, uncovered, for about 1½ hours. Strain stock and discard the bones and flesh (or save for the cat). Sprinkle chopped parsley on top before serving. Makes 6 servings.

❊ Cold Shrimp Soup ❊

Pieter Kelder introduces the first course: "Initiates refer to this as my 'buttermilk' soup, but I have found that, unfortunately, the word buttermilk carries a lot of sales resistance." Hence the change of name. You can use canned shrimp, too, but the fresh shrimp gives a boost to the flavor.

2 medium-sized cucumbers, peeled, then grated
3 tablespoons prepared mustard
1 teaspoon prepared horseradish
1 teaspoon salt
1 teaspoon sugar
About 1 cup shelled and deveined cooked shrimp
1 quart buttermilk
1 tablespoon chopped chives

Combine all ingredients but the chives and place in refrigerator for at least 4 to 6 hours before serving. Blend in chopped chives just before serving.

Makes 4 to 6 servings.

For a luncheon main course, you might double or even triple the amount of shrimp.

ৠ Onion Soup...with Shallots ৠ

Cecil J. Geraghty proposes a fine simple recipe for onion soup—but he makes it with shallots. And the trouble is that quite a few people don't know what shallots are.

The shallot (*Allium ascalonicum*), the onion (*A. cepa*), and the leek (*A. porrum*) are all closely related. However, the shallot is least likely to be available. Actually you could use green onions, or even leeks, pretty well in the same recipe.

1 ¼ cups thinly sliced young green shallots
¼ cup (½ cube) butter
6 cups hot water
6 bouillon cubes
1 loaf French bread
Butter
Parmesan cheese
Salt to taste

This exquisite delicacy is prepared as follows:

Obtain a few shallots from a friend and plant them in your garden. When they have matured, divide them and replant the corms, repeating as often as necessary to make a fair-sized stand of shallots.

When the green shallots are again about the thickness of your finger, pick a good fistful or two and clean them (resisting the temptation to eat them raw). Slice thinly, using all the lighter green portions.

Now melt some butter in a saucepan and sauté the sliced shallots, using only enough heat so you can barely hear the sizzle. Let them brown to about the degree of caramelization that occurs when your wife lets the vegetables boil dry but serves them anyway.

Now add hot water in an amount appropriate to whatever is your idea of what onion soup should be, and add about a cube of bouillon for each cup of water. Let this simmer for as long as you can stand to wait, but at least half an hour.

While the soup simmers, slice a loaf of French bread, spread slices with butter and Parmesan cheese and toast in the oven. Put a slice of toast in each bowl, and pour the soup over. Serve with the rest of the toast and more Parmesan cheese. Let each diner salt the soup to his own taste. Makes 6 servings.

Too bad this can't be prepared more quickly, but there's no other way to obtain a dependable supply of green shallots.

⚙ Memorable Okra Gumbo ⚙

Truly memorable recipes often relate to one's total experience, flashes of memory, streams of consciousness.

"This recipe," says Benjamin Torres, Jr., "is an outcome of three streams: 1) a mother who thought all her children—including sons—ought to know how to cook well, 2) lingering memories of taste-tantalizers during two visits through Louisiana, 3) a 2½-year-old son who could never get enough okra in a commercially canned chicken gumbo."

The green mucilaginous pods of the tall African herb called okra don't suit everybody's taste. But many have found it most to their liking when surrounded by all the other pleasant trappings of the typical Louisiana-style gumbo.

6 cups chicken broth (or 6 cups water and 4
chicken bouillon cubes)
1 cup diced cooked ham (bone optional)
½ cup diced cooked chicken (optional)
¼ teaspoon whole thyme
1 bay leaf
1 small, dried, hot chile pepper
½ cup sliced celery
½ cup diced onion
1 medium-sized tomato, diced
1 package (10 oz.) frozen okra, partially thawed
3 tablespoons salad oil
2 tablespoons flour
1 can (4½ oz.) shrimp, rinsed and drained
Steamed rice
Gumbo filé powder (available at
most spice counters)
Liquid hot-pepper seasoning (optional)

In a pan that can be covered, combine broth, ham, chicken (if used), thyme, bay leaf, chile pepper, celery, onion, and tomato. Bring to a boil, then reduce heat, cover, and allow to simmer about 10 minutes. Cut okra into ½-inch-thick pieces and sauté in salad oil over medium heat 5 minutes. Sprinkle flour over okra, stir to mix in, and simmer 5 minutes; set aside.

About 5 minutes before serving soup, remove chile and bay leaf. Add okra and shrimp; cook just until heated through and okra is tender.

Partially fill individual soup bowls with hot steamed rice. Ladle gumbo over rice. Sprinkle gumbo filé powder to taste on top. A dash of the liquid hot-pepper seasoning may be added. Makes 6 to 8 servings.

⚛ Marrow Balls for Soup ⚛

"What is more satisfying than a bowl of good, clear, hot soup with mouthwatering marrow balls floating in same?" asks Clayton Horn.

Though much neglected in these steak-or-nothing days, marrow is good food, available for the asking. There are various recipes for marrow balls (one cook book lists them under "soup accessories"—do you want to accessorize your soup?), but none specify parsley and nutmeg seasoning, or the neat trick of pre-freezing. One partaker calls these "a nice cross between dumplings and croutons."

2 tablespoons marrow
4 tablespoons cracker or bread crumbs
1 egg
1 teaspoon finely chopped parsley
¾ teaspoon salt
⅛ teaspoon pepper
⅛ teaspoon nutmeg
Clear soup stock, mildly seasoned

Have your meatman split up lengthwise an 8 to 10-inch beef shank bone. Scoop out and measure 2 tablespoons marrow (freeze any extra). Mash and mix marrow with crumbs, egg, parsley, and seasonings. Place in refrigerator long enough to chill. Remove and roll between the hands (a slight dusting of flour on the hands will help) to form balls about 1 inch in diameter. Chill the marrow balls (or store in freezer for future use).

Bring soup to slow boil; then drop in chilled or frozen marrow balls. As soon as they rise to the top, they are hot, cooked, and ready to serve.

The recipe makes 12 to 15 marrow balls, enough for 4 to 6 servings.

⚛ Hot Weather, Cold Borscht ⚛

"A cold beet borscht is most welcome when the temperature soars," says Mervin Mathias, M.D., emphatically.

The Society for the Encouragement of Cold Soups (SECS) highly endorses his contribution. Yet be warned that tomato has crept in, to the possible consternation of some of the borscht boosters. Play it cagily and taste first, if the ratio of tomato to beet flavor is very important to you. On the other hand, there may be just as many to cheer for less beet and more tomato, thank you.

1 can (1 lb.) julienne, diced, or sliced beets
About ½ can (8-oz. size) tomato sauce
2½ cups water
1 teaspoon salt
½ teaspoon sugar, or to taste
1 medium-sized onion
Juice of ½ lemon, or to taste
Sour cream

Combine beets, tomato sauce, water, salt, and sugar. Quarter the onion, cutting almost but not entirely through; add to soup. Bring to a boil and then simmer slowly for 30 minutes, covered. (Some of the beets can be mashed to thicken the borscht, if you wish.) Remove onion, chill, then add lemon juice. Serve with a dollop of sour cream on top of each serving, or mix it thoroughly with each serving. Makes 4 servings.

❊ Hot-or-Cold Cucumber Soup ❊

Bob Blair is well known as a talented cook in his home town. His recipe for Cucumber Soup lives up to his reputation. A small minority may recommend straining out some of the larger cucumber seeds.

2 cups coarsely chopped cucumbers
1 cup light cream
1 cup chicken broth
¼ cup chopped chives
¼ cup chopped celery leaves
3 sprigs parsley
1 tablespoon soft butter
1 tablespoon flour
Salt and pepper to taste
Chopped dill (or finely chopped cucumber and grated lemon rind)

Put all ingredients except the salt and pepper and the dill (or cucumber and lemon rind) in a blender. Blend until smooth (cover your blender or you will be cleaning your ceiling). Remove to saucepan and place over low heat until soup reaches a boil. Season with salt and pepper. Garnish with chopped dill and serve hot, or garnish with finely chopped cucumber and grated lemon rind and serve cold. Makes about 6 to 8 servings.

❊ The World's Best Hash ❊

"My wife—no mean cook herself—says this is the world's best hash. You will notice that it uses raw potatoes and cooks the onion very little, the principal secrets of its great success."

One might be tempted to tone down the title of Navy Captain Robert D. Phillips' creation perhaps to "One of the World's Two Great Hashes." However, it is quite good enough to justify a little bragging.

You may have noticed that it is practically impossible to make a hash that will satisfy everybody; for one thing, they divide quite sharply into those who like hash dry and those who like it moist. But this one comes mighty close to satisfying both groups. The directions indicate how closely you must watch the whole process.

1½ quarts diced (about ½-inch cubes) cooked roast beef
1½ quarts finely diced (¼-inch cubes) raw potatoes
½ cup flour
2 tablespoons bacon fat
2 tablespoons salad oil or butter
2 medium-sized onions
Salt and pepper to taste

You must have a piece of cooked roast beef to start with, which you will cut up into small pieces. *Do not grind.* Cut the potatoes into rather fine dice, dry them on paper towels, and sprinkle with flour.

Put the bacon fat and oil in a warm iron frying pan (Bob can't vouch for good hash in any other kind, but use something else if you have to). When the fats have heated, put in the floured potatoes and brown slowly, turning when necessary. Test the potatoes for doneness by tasting, and when they are very nearly cooked through, add thinly sliced onion, turning it in so that it becomes warmed and wilted but *not* soft.

Add the meat at the very end so that it is just barely warmed through (it should not be cooked until it falls apart and becomes stringy). Never cover the hash; greasiness and steaminess will result. Add more bacon fat or oil if you need it, but use as little as possible. Makes 6 servings.

You can put catsup or homemade chile sauce on the table, but it is unlikely that anyone will use it.

﹡ Bonanza Spinach Soup ﹡

In his "small dinner house," Ludington Patton does the cooking one day a week when the rest of the crew is off. "I like to add a different, special soup and have, on occasion, served mushroom bisque, parsnip or olive soup, borscht, vichyssoise, and most recently, one I call Bonanza Spinach Soup, which was concocted at the last minute and turned out to be a success worth repeating."

It is green, naturally, and thick without being creamy. The vaguely mint-like aftertaste could easily become too bitter if you add the rosemary too freely. If you cool it after cooking, this should be a good soup to serve cold.

"A blender is necessary to get the right consistency," Ludington insists.

½ pound sliced bacon
½ teaspoon fresh rosemary leaves
2 bunches fresh spinach, well washed
and drained
1 large onion, sliced
Cayenne
Salt and pepper
1 quart milk (approximately)

Cook bacon in large frying pan until crisp; drain off all but about 2 tablespoons of the drippings. Add rosemary leaves, spinach, and onion; toss with bacon until cooked through. Put mixture in blender until smooth. Add seasonings to taste. Add milk to desired thickness of soup. Blend again, correct seasoning, remove to saucepan, and heat to serving temperature. Makes 6 servings.

﹡ Lentil Soup ﹡

Simple and direct is Don Normark's Lentil Soup, also "good after a football game." Try to serve it at a time when it doesn't have to compete with more sophisticated flavors. Then lovers of the lentil will enjoy it to the full, and others will feel more kindly disposed toward this lowly legume.

2 cups lentils
6 cups water
½ pound salt pork, cubed
1 big onion, diced very fine
1 or 2 bay leaves
¼ teaspoon oregano
1 large clove garlic
Piece of pepperoni about the diameter of
a 50-cent piece and about 6 inches long,
cut into paper-thin slices

Soak lentils in the water for 1 hour (or if you forget to soak, just cook soup a little longer than specified). Fry salt pork until crisp, then pour off all but 3 or 4 tablespoons of fat. Add all remaining ingredients to fat and sizzle until golden brown. Bring lentils to a boil in water in which they were soaked. Add onion-pepperoni mixture and simmer until lentils are tender —from 1 to 2 hours.

Serve hot. This can be a full meal if you add fruit salad, crusty bread, and coffee. Makes 8 servings.

Morning-after Menudo

"This soup, according to Mexican tradition and personal experience, is very good medicine for too much 'night before' and makes you *muy fuerte*."

In this testimonial fashion does William Buster McGee, M.D., begin his gastronomical prescription.

Menudo is a time-honored Mexican remedy for hangover. Some take it as a preventive before the infirmity sets in, stopping into some all-night cafe to top off a convivial evening with a bowl of menudo at 4 or 5 A.M., then going home to sleep like babes.

Throughout most of Mexico, the ingredients are more or less standard (if you remember that Mexicans don't care much for standardization). They include tripe, calves' feet, corn in some form (usually nixtamal in Mexico, but Americans may use hominy, and Bill substitutes garbanzos), chopped onion, garlic, chile, oregano; and a squeeze of lime goes well with any soup in Mexico.

The milder ingredients will tend to soothe you, but there are also small touches of violence. Not everyone will like the tripe. (Not all Mexicans like it either.) However Bill thoughtfully writes a do-it-yourself prescription consisting of a basic formula plus a formidable list of optional ingredients that tend to make the tripe less dominant.

The effect of adding all the optional ingredients is good, but certain ones, such as the peanut butter or the olives, could be omitted and you would scarcely miss them. Therefore the best advice is to make the basic soup, taste it, then add from the optional list those ingredients that intrigue you most.

BASIC RECIPE

3 pounds honeycomb beef tripe, cut into
1½-inch squares
2 beef shanks with meat on them
6 pigs' feet
2 cans (about 1 lb. each) garbanzos
1 tablespoon salt
4 to 6 tablespoons chile powder
2 onions, finely chopped
4 cloves garlic, mashed or minced
1 large can (1 lb., 12 oz.) tomatoes
1 can (10½ oz.) consommé
1 can (10½ oz.) bouillon
1 quart water

OPTIONAL INGREDIENTS

1 tablespoon oregano
½ teaspoon liquid hot-pepper seasoning
2 cups chopped ham
1 pound mushrooms, sliced
½ pound chorizo, removed from casings
4 tablespoons peanut butter
2 cans (7½ oz. each) pitted ripe olives
1 quart beer (substituted for water in basic recipe)
Juice of 3 lemons

Combine all ingredients in basic recipe, bring to a boil, then reduce and simmer slowly for 8 hours. Add optional ingredients of your choice (except for beer, which would have to go in at the beginning) about 30 minutes before cooking is completed. Let soup cool enough to remove all bones. Reheat to serve. One final option is to serve with finely chopped green onions, including tops. Makes about 4 quarts soup.

Hangover Stew

Taking the bull by the horns is appropriate to some circumstances, but F. P. Cronemiller prefers to take him by the tail. Once it is firmly grasped, he plunges this tail with one or two others into a cauldron of boiling beer to produce a very respectable beef stew.

The name of chef Cronemiller's dish is Hangover Stew, on which he hangs another tale: "Coming out of a logging camp one morning after a night in which there had been a little over-indulgence, I knew some food would help. As I went past a little hole-in-the-wall restaurant, I noticed a black-board on which one item was 'Beef Stew'. The entrepreneur-owner-cook-waiter told me the recipe suited my indisposition and that he had quite a large clientele for it. It went about like this recipe (or, at least, this is the way I now make it)."

          2 pounds oxtails, cut up
          1 quart beer
     1 or 2 onions, quartered
     1 or 2 carrots, quartered
          ½ teaspoon rosemary
          1 tablespoon Worcestershire
         10 drops brown bottled gravy sauce
          1 clove garlic, minced or mashed
          1 teaspoon salt, or to taste
          ½ teaspoon pepper, or to taste
          2 small potatoes, quartered

Put meat in kettle; cover well with beer (and set remaining beer, if any, to one side for separate consumption). Bring things to a boil and simmer slowly for 1½ hours, or until you can start pulling the meat from the bone with a fork. Add onion, carrot, and all the seasoning and continue simmering for 15 minutes. Add potato and simmer 30 minutes longer, or until ingredients are about to fall apart but don't. (You may thicken soup with a small amount of flour or cornstarch, if you wish.) Makes about 4 servings.

ᴹ S.O.B. Stew ᴹ

This is not a beef stew exactly, but sort of a son-of-a-beef stew. It developed in our Southwest cow camps, says F. P. Cronemiller. "Animals were slaughtered on the range, and the first night, while the carcass cooled, a stew was made of the innards.

"As for the name: In the old days, cowboys often preferred an unprintable name for places and things to a decent one. This stew is supposed to have originated in a cow camp that had run out of meat and salt, with two weeks to go on the roundup; so an animal was killed and his innards went into the pot. The first cowboy to taste the resulting flat, saltless mixture came out with the name, and it stuck."

Chef Cronemiller suggests the original cow country cooking method of burying a cast iron pot in a pit filled with hot coals. But a Dutch oven in the kitchen offers more control over final results.

¼ cup chopped beef suet or shortening
½ pound beef heart
½ pound kidney
½ pound butcher's steak (hanging tenderloin)
2 medium-sized onions, sliced
1 teaspoon salt
¼ teaspoon pepper
¼ teaspoon liquid hot-pepper seasoning
3 cups water
4 medium-sized carrots, sliced
4 medium-sized potatoes, cut in large cubes
½ pound sweetbreads (optional)
½ pound brains (optional)

Render the suet in a Dutch oven. Cut beef heart, kidney, and butcher's steak into 1-inch cubes; sauté in fat until lightly browned. Add onion, salt, pepper, liquid hot-pepper seasoning, and water. Cover and cook in a slow oven (300°) for 1½ hours. Remove from oven, stir well, add carrots and potatoes; return to oven for 2 more hours, or until fork-tender.

Meanwhile, parboil sweetbreads and brains, if used, in boiling water for 10 minutes. During last 15 minutes of cooking time, add the sweetbreads and brains to the stew. Taste, and add more salt and pepper if needed. Serve in large bowls with plenty of crusty bread. Makes 6 to 8 servings, depending on number of innards used.

❀ Cream of Coconut Soup Kahala ❀

There's something very sustaining and satisfying about a coconut soup, in case you've never tasted one. As proof, just eavesdrop on some diners as they thoughtfully "chew" Cream of Coconut Soup Kahala, as designed by Max Wilhelm, of Honolulu:

"Slightly sweet and spicy . . . nice blend . . . no one flavor predominates, except coconut—ever so slightly . . . subtle . . . creamy consistency . . . almost curry-like . . . cloves add an elusive bit of flavor . . . pale green-gold color . . . nice coconut overtone."

Frozen coconut milk in 1-pint containers is getting more plentiful in the specialty food stores of larger metropolitan areas. But if you can't locate any, just make your own for this recipe: In a blender, combine 5 cups packaged flaked coconut and 5 cups milk. Chill 1 hour. Then whirl in blender at high speed for about 10 seconds and pour through a fine wire strainer, pressing out as much liquid as possible.

1 onion, diced
2 leeks, diced
1 celery stalk, diced
2 cloves
1 bay leaf
½ cup (1 cube) butter
1 cup rice flour
3 quarts chicken stock
1 quart frozen coconut milk, thawed
½ pint (1 cup) heavy cream
Salt and pepper to taste
Nutmeg to taste

Sauté onion, leeks, celery, cloves, and bay leaf in butter but do not brown. Add rice flour and mix well. Add boiling chicken stock and coconut milk; stir well and simmer approximately 30 minutes. If soup gets too thick, add some more chicken stock. Strain the soup, add cream and seasonings. Makes 10 servings.

❀ Veal Beerstew ❀

Glen M. Hodges' offers a tasty veal stew in which there are a couple of surprises, notably the beer and salted peanuts. But it got a favorable reaction from one consumer who said, "With a little salt, this just approaches greatness."

2½ cups beer
1 package (amount for 4 to 6 servings) onion soup mix
¼ cup salad oil
2 cloves garlic, peeled and halved
1½ pounds boneless veal stew meat
Flour
½ cup chopped parsley
6 large fresh mushrooms, or 1 can (3 or 4 oz.) mushrooms, drained
¼ cup chopped salted peanuts
2 tablespoons butter
Freshly ground pepper
Salt (optional)
3 cups hot cooked rice or noodles

Bring the beer to a boil and add onion soup mix. Simmer about 10 minutes. Meanwhile, heat oil in a frying pan and sauté garlic until golden. Remove garlic. Dredge veal stew meat in flour and sauté in garlic oil until golden.

Add the meat to the beer mixture together with parsley, cover, and simmer very gently until meat is tender (about ½ hour). Just before meat is done, sauté sliced mushrooms and peanuts in butter and add to meat just before serving. Add pepper to taste and salt if necessary. Serve the stew over rice or noodles. Makes 4 servings.

❧ German White Bean Soup ❧

C. O. Ritter suggests a German bean soup rich with ham, and also thick with white beans and decorative with a quantity of green ones. He explains its background thus:

"This recipe is at least 75 or 100 years old in its basic form. When I was a child this was the way leftover ham shank was used, and I must say we all looked forward to baked ham more for the soup than for the initial meals. You had better have your appetite honed, since seconds are always the order of the day.

"If you serve this with fresh French bread, I'll guarantee that you'll have a rebuttal for those who believe soup is just a starter."

2 cups (about 1 lb.) Great Northern white beans
2 lean smoked ham hocks (about 2 lbs.)
1 teaspoon seasoned pepper
2 bay leaves
About 5 quarts water
3 packages (9 oz. each) frozen green beans,
partially thawed
Salt

Wash white beans and place in 8-quart pan. Add ham hocks, seasoned pepper, bay leaves, and water. Bring to a boil over high heat, then reduce heat and simmer until beans are tender and liquid is cream-colored (about 3 hours). Add water as needed to replenish that absorbed by beans. Remove meat from ham hocks and return meat to soup. Discard bone and fat. Add green beans and salt to taste. Continue to simmer until frozen beans are tender, about 15 minutes. Serve with buttered French bread. Makes about 6 quarts.

❧ Oft-Requested Salmon Chowder ❧

"I have been making this fish chowder since 1918 when I was up in Alaska salmon fishing for the canneries," says Alfred Lindahn. "Up there I used only the salmon bellies, and oh what a rich chowder that was. My family often requests this dish."

Fred is right; this is a glorious thing to do with salmon.

1½ pounds salmon
1 sprig or pinch thyme
1 sprig or pinch tarragon
2 quarts water
2 slices bacon
2 onions, finely chopped
2 sprigs parsley, finely chopped
3 carrots, finely chopped
3 or 4 medium-sized potatoes, finely chopped
1 stalk celery, finely chopped
1 cube beef bouillon (optional)
Salt and pepper
1 can (1 lb.) tomatoes
1 can (7 oz.) minced clams

Simmer salmon with thyme and tarragon in water until salmon flakes easily, about 15 minutes. Remove salmon; discard bones and skin. Strain stock and reserve. Cook bacon, onions, and parsley together until limp, about 5 minutes; add to stock. Bring stock to boil and add carrots, potatoes, celery, bouillon cube, and salt and pepper to taste. Cook until vegetables are done, about 15 minutes. Add tomatoes, clams, salmon; simmer an additional 10 minutes. Makes 4 to 6 meal-sized servings.

TO FILL A SWEET TOOTH

As far as many adults are concerned, desserts aren't what they used to be. Even men who don't have the will power to pass up dessert when it comes with the full-course dinner in a restaurant can be Spartan about skipping it or at least skimping on it at home.

If and when dessert is allowed, the most allowable form is fruit. It gives that certain sweetness many people yearn for at the end of a meal, yet it is low in the units that add all that poundage.

In this collection of recipes, the largest number consists of fruit, plus just enough sweetening or liqueur or spice or other flavoring to make the fruit seem something extra special. Next are the puddings, about half of which use fruit as a major ingredient. Trailing well behind in this particular popularity poll are pies, cakes, and cookies—the desserts that used to dominate our menus and the ones that are still traditional.

As a special concession to tradition and for old times' sake, this chapter contains not only a holiday fruitcake but also a holiday mincemeat.

⚒ Fresh Pears Bordelaise ⚒

Appropriate to the season of harvest and to the holidays are the bright red Pears Bordelaise which Frank McNally cooks by "a traditional family recipe." If you start with pears that aren't fully ripe, they may be hard to eat with a spoon, in which case you might try coring them.

8 ripe, firm pears
2 cups Cabernet Sauvignon wine
1 cup sugar
½ teaspoon vanilla
A 1-inch stick of cinnamon
4 whole cloves

Remove skin from pears; leave stems on. Combine wine, sugar, vanilla, cinnamon, and cloves. Bring to a rolling boil, drop in the pears, reduce heat, and simmer until pears are tender—but not mushy—and rose-hued. Carefully remove pears, place in individual dessert dishes, and chill. Cook liquid down to syrup consistency. Pour over the chilled pears and serve or serve ice cold the next day. Makes 8 servings.

⚒ Brandy Sauce for All Seasons ⚒

Donald Torrence proposes his Brandy Sauce "for your favorite holiday pudding," but there's no need to abstain from it between holidays. Pour some over any pudding or plain ice cream, or let a batch cool and try it over fresh or cooked fruit.

2 to 2¼ cups powdered sugar
6 tablespoons butter
2¼ cups half-and-half (half milk, half cream)
2 eggs, slightly beaten
1 teaspoon lemon juice
¼ to ½ cup brandy (to taste)

Mix sugar, butter, and half-and-half in a heavy saucepan and slowly bring to a boil, stirring constantly. Remove from heat and stir in the slightly beaten eggs. Return to heat and continue to stir until the mixture again boils. Remove at once and add lemon juice and brandy. Do not boil again after brandy has been added, but the sauce can be reheated as necessary. Makes about 3½ cups sauce.

✖ Pineapple-Cheese Pudding Cake ✖

Something for the sweet tooth? Frederick Schabel is your man. He doesn't believe in doing these things on too small a scale—you'll be in the kitchen quite a while. But the children, and most of the grownups, too, will be smacking their lips.

1 cup graham cracker crumbs (about 15 squares)
⅓ cup melted butter
3 tablespoons sugar
½ teaspoon nutmeg
12 ounces cream cheese
⅔ cup sweetened condensed milk
3 large eggs, separated
⅓ cup sour cream
2 tablespoons powdered sugar
1 teaspoon vanilla
½ teaspoon grated lemon peel
1 can (about 14 oz.) crushed pineapple,
    well drained
¼ teaspoon salt
¼ teaspoon cream of tartar
6 tablespoons apricot jam
2 tablespoons rum
Powdered sugar

Combine cracker crumbs, butter, sugar, and nutmeg, and spread out in an even layer on the bottom of a 9-inch spring form pan.

Have cream cheese at room temperature; beat until fluffy; blend in sweetened condensed milk. Beat in egg yolks one at a time. Beat in sour cream, sugar, vanilla, and lemon peel. Stir in drained pineapple. Add salt and cream of tartar to egg whites; beat until soft peaks form. Fold egg whites into cheese mixture. Turn into pan on top of crumb crust. Bake in a slow oven (300°) about 40 minutes, or until almost set in center. Cool in pan, then refrigerate.

When the cake is cold, heat apricot jam and rum together just until boiling; brush over top of cake. When jam mixture has cooled, dust top with powdered sugar. Makes 16 servings.

✖ Strawberries in Port ✖

"Strawberries in Port" has an elegant sound. Duane Spurling suggests pouring the mixture over shortcake or ice cream; it's also good just plain at the end of a heavy meal. One sipper commented: "I did enjoy that juice."

3 cups sliced strawberries
3 tablespoons sugar
1 cup port wine

Place berries in shallow bowl and sprinkle with sugar. Add wine and then refrigerate at least 2 or as long as 6 hours, stirring occasionally. Serve alone or over ice cream, shortcake, pound cake, or any plain cake. Makes 4 servings.

❊ Ginger-ly Pears ❊

Loosen your necktie, roll up your sleeves, and work off your tensions on this recipe from A. E. Hobson. It has class, but isn't pretentious.

The topping is virtually flawless. But if you want this dessert easy to eat, the pears should be spoon ripe. Otherwise, you may prefer to simmer them just until tender in a very light syrup with perhaps a touch of ginger added. Then add the topping and take spoon in hand.

8 Comice pears, peeled, halved, and cored

SAUCE

1 egg, well beaten
1 cup powdered sugar
3 tablespoons melted butter
¼ teaspoon ginger
1 teaspoon grated lemon peel
2 tablespoons rum, or rum flavoring to taste
1 cup whipping cream, whipped

Arrange pear halves on plates, two per serving. Top with the sauce (preferably made 3 or 4 hours ahead of time and then kept in the refrigerator while the flavors mingle). To make the sauce, simply combine all ingredients except cream, then carefully fold it in last. Makes 8 servings.

❊ Golden Zabaglione ❊

There are people who are for zabaglione, and there are those who are against it. If you like it, this is the egg at one of its finest moments, whipped to a golden froth, lightly sweetened, redolent of fine wine. Henry George Watkins says: "It has been my experience that most zabaglione is too sweet or the wine used too heavy for my palate. Hence my variation." The variation is primarily in the use of equal parts sherry and sauterne, instead of a heavier wine such as the classic Marsala.

6 egg yolks
5 tablespoons sugar
¼ cup dry sherry
¼ cup sauterne

Combine yolks with sugar in the top of a double boiler. Add wine, and beat together using a wire whip. Place over water that is barely bubbling, and whip constantly until mixture leaves a trail behind the whip, about 5 minutes. Serve immediately. Makes 4 servings.

⚶ Sherbet Mandarin ⚶

Alfred W. Cherry speaks for his recipe:

"This one is far too simple to be that good. But it is.

"It was served once after an awesome meal. We were full, and we were tired. It seemed right to finish the repast with something very light and a little sweet.

"On a hunch, we threw two parts together and got something a great deal more than the sum."

1 scoop orange sherbet
About 1 tablespoon canned Mandarin oranges

Cover sherbet with drained mandarin oranges and serve. That's all there is to it. Makes 1 serving.

⚶ Oatmeal Fruit Cookies ⚶

"When a bachelor starts in on a recipe, something is bound to happen. This time it was good," reports William Goe.

"It" is an oatmeal cooky, delightfully loaded with the kind of goodies we tend to associate with Christmas—fruits and nuts and sugars and spices. The honey, peanut butter, and dried fruits, in particular, give it a good moist consistency. The outside bakes crisp but the interior remains a little cake-like.

One of the cooky-jar crowd called these "nice, lumpy little cookies"—and meant it as a compliment.

½ cup seedless raisins
⅓ cup shortening
½ cup sugar
3 tablespoons honey
4 teaspoons peanut butter
1 egg, well beaten
1 cup flour
¼ teaspoon salt
¼ teaspoon soda
¼ teaspoon cinnamon
¼ teaspoon cloves
¼ teaspoon ginger
5 teaspoons milk
1 teaspoon vanilla
½ cup quick cooking rolled oats
⅓ cup mixed candied fruit
⅓ cup finely chopped walnuts
⅓ cup moist-pack prunes, cut in small pieces

Pour boiling water over raisins, let stand 5 minutes, drain, and dry on paper towels. Cream shortening and sugar together thoroughly. Blend in honey and peanut butter. Add beaten egg and mix well. Sift flour, measure, and sift with salt, soda, cinnamon, cloves, and ginger. Blend flour mixture into cream mixture alternately with milk. Stir in all remaining ingredients. Drop by tablespoonfuls on cooky sheet, flatten slightly, and bake in a moderately hot oven (375°) from 8 to 12 minutes. Makes 4 dozen cookies.

❧ Western Angel Pie ❧

Angel Pie is more than a term of endearment in Max J. Kuney's book of recipes. It's a dessert that even the nothing-but-fruit-and-cheese school will find hard to resist. "Pure wonderful," says one fan.

CRUST

4 egg whites
¼ teaspoon cream of tartar
1 cup sugar
½ teaspoon vanilla extract

FILLING

12 egg yolks
1½ cups sugar
Juice of 3 lemons (½ cup)

TOPPING

½ pint whipping cream
1 cup sliced almonds, toasted

Beat egg whites until bubbly; add cream of tartar. Continue beating, adding sugar one teaspoon at a time and vanilla one drop at a time until smooth and satiny. Spread in well buttered 9-inch pie pan and bake in a very slow oven (275°) for 10 minutes; lower heat to 250° and continue baking for 40 minutes. Cool in refrigerator.

For the filling, beat egg yolks until thick in the top of a double boiler. Place over hot water and add sugar and lemon juice; cook until thick, beating continually. Remove from heat. While mixture cools, beat at intervals to keep smooth. When cool, pour into the baked pie shell and refrigerate.

When pie is chilled, whip cream until thick and spread on top. Sprinkle on toasted almonds and refrigerate until serving time. Makes 6 servings.

❧ French Quarter Bananas ❧

"I do all the cooking at our house," says Vern Lanegrasse, "because I like to try new recipes and also like to try ol' recipes from my forefathers in New Orleans. Here is a dessert from there, so simple to fix, yet at a dinner party it impresses."

The dish is dramatic, and since bananas cook so quickly, it requires only a few minutes' preparation just before serving time.

2 tablespoons butter
4 teaspoons brown sugar
2 bananas
⅛ teaspoon cinnamon
1 teaspoon banana liqueur
1 ounce rum or brandy
Vanilla ice cream

Mix butter and sugar in a chafing dish or saucepan. Cook over medium heat until medium dark brown, about 3 minutes. Cut bananas in quarters or slice, add to butter and sugar, and heat until well coated with the sauce, about 2 minutes. Add cinnamon and liqueur; stir. Remove from heat and add rum or brandy to top of mixture; *do not stir!* Flame, and spoon over 6 individual servings of ice cream while still flaming.

⚛ Fruit-Full Fruitcake ⚛

H. G. Watkins is one who has always favored a really fruity fruitcake. The one he proposes here may be just as caloric as the other kind, but it may give you a certain reassurance to say, "This is really more fruit than cake."

½ pound candied cherries
½ pound seedless golden raisins
¼ pound citron
¼ pound dried white figs
¼ pound candied apricots (recipe follows)
2 ounces candied orange peel
2 ounces candied lemon peel
1 cup brandy
2 cups regular all-purpose flour
1 teaspoon baking powder
¼ teaspoon salt
1½ teaspoons cinnamon
1½ teaspoons allspice
1½ teaspoons nutmeg
1½ teaspoons mace
½ cup (1 cube) butter or margarine
1 cup brown sugar, firmly packed
2 eggs, separated
⅓ cup honey
1 pound coarsely broken walnuts
1 jar (8 oz.) orange marmalade
Brandy for keeping cake moist

Cut fruit in fairly large pieces, mix with the 1 cup brandy, and let stand 12 hours or more in a covered container, stirring occasionally. Sift flour, measure, then sift with baking powder, salt, cinnamon, allspice, nutmeg, and mace. Cream together the butter and sugar until light and fluffy. Blend in well beaten egg yolks, then honey. Add sifted dry ingredients and the nuts and marmalade. Fold in stiffly beaten egg whites. Finally add the brandy-soaked fruits.

Turn into a greased and floured 10-inch tube pan. Bake in a very slow oven (250°) about 5½ hours. Keep a pan of water on the bottom of the oven; remove during the last hour of baking. (If you bake this in smaller loaves, allow 2½ hours for a 1-pound loaf, or 3½ hours for a 2-pound loaf.) This recipe yields approximately 5 pounds cake. When the cake is done, remove from oven and cool in pan for about

20 minutes. Remove from pan and cool completely on a cake rack. Take a piece of cheesecloth or clean linen large enough to wrap around the fruitcake, and moisten with brandy (the cloth should be thoroughly moistened, but not wringing wet).

Wrap the fruitcake in the cloth and store in a crock or other closed container. It will taste best if it can age a month or more. Every few days check the dampness of the cloth, and moisten with a little more brandy when it begins to dry.

Candied Apricots

To ¼ pound dried apricots, add ½ cup honey. Place in a pan, cover, and simmer until apricot halves appear semiclear. Let cool, spread out to dry, then handle as you would any other candied fruit.

⚶ Plum Pudding Brandy Sauce ⚶

Very high marks go to Dr. Russell H. Huff for this pudding sauce. Says he, "This Scandinavian recipe has been in our family for three generations, and I feel that it is one of the finest of pudding sauces. It is especially delicious with plum pudding."

It is recommendable for any kind of holiday pudding. The mixture is definitely rich, and creamy, yet simple and somehow light in effect. The brandy flavor is quite subtle, so much so that abstainers will find this an excellent sauce even without adding the brandy.

1 cup sugar
½ cup (1 cube) butter
4 egg yolks, well beaten
1 cup warmed whipping cream
2 to 3 tablespoons brandy

Cream together the sugar and butter. Add egg yolks and cream and beat well. Place in a double boiler and cook to the consistency of heavy cream, but do not overcook. Add brandy and pour sauce over pudding. Serve warm or cold. Makes about 2½ cups sauce.

⚶ Coffee Marshmallow Mousse ⚶

A recipe conceived by a man containing only three ingredients? Seems hard to believe, but here it is, from Louis H. Prince, who says:

"Although a long-transplanted Southerner (35 years in the Pacific Northwest), I nevertheless tend to cling to the 'eatments of my raisin'. This dessert, an authentic Southern delicacy, is not only simple to prepare but also has a character of flavor that appeals to Yankee and Southerners alike."

This is one refrigerator dessert that seems to freeze to a just-right consistency, neither too soft nor too hard. It is rich but simple. The coffee that goes in can be just about as strong as you feel like making it.

1 cup strong coffee (can be made with
instant coffee)
20 standard-sized marshmallows
½ pint whipping cream

Pour coffee into saucepan, add marshmallows, and heat, stirring gently, until marshmallows have melted. Cool this mixture until it begins to set. Whip cream until stiff, and fold into coffee-marshmallow mixture. Transfer to refrigerator trays and let stand in refrigerator until frozen. Makes 4 to 6 servings.

✂ Firehouse Date Pudding ✂

People don't usually think of firemen as cooks, but it's easy to see why cooking might be a desirable accomplishment for them.

"In San Francisco firehouses, all firemen take turns cooking on their shift," says A. E. Hobson (hoseman, "40 Engine"). "I have found when I cook that this is the most popular dessert I can make. It's good and can be eaten hot or cold, which, as you know can be important to us."

Although this dish has certainly survived its trial by fire, test it yourself and prove it. It could really be called either a pudding or a cake. You may favor adding a topping of whipped cream, lemon sauce, or vanilla ice cream.

1½ cups flour
¼ teaspoon baking powder
¼ teaspoon salt
1 cup chopped nut meats
1 package (8 oz.) pitted dates
1 teaspoon soda
1 cup boiling water
¼ cup butter
1 cup sugar
1 egg
Grated peel ½ lemon

Preheat oven to 300°. Sift flour, measure, and sift with baking powder and salt, and then mix in nuts. Cut up dates, mix soda into them, pour over boiling water, and let stand. Meanwhile, cream butter until soft, add sugar, and then beat in egg very well. Combine flour and butter mixtures. Finally stir in date and soda mixture and add grated lemon. Put in a 9-inch-square baking pan, well greased, and bake 1 hour. Cool in pan and cut into squares. Serve warm with whipped cream, or frost and eat cold as cake. Makes 6 to 8 servings.

✂ Chewy Fruit Bars ✂

These cookies are hearty, chewy, spicy, fruity. They get their texture from the dried fruit. They are attractive in shape, being cut on the diagonal. The fruit makes them get more moist as they age. "Good keepers if you don't have a lot of children around," says Moise Penning. (And good nourishers if you do.)

¾ cup shortening
2¼ cups sugar
2 eggs
½ cup molasses
½ cup water
1 teaspoon vanilla
1 tablespoon cinnamon
½ teaspoon nutmeg
¼ teaspoon mace
1 teaspoon salt
1 teaspoon soda
6 cups flour
1½ pounds dried fruit—prunes, dates, apricots, any mixture of your choice
1½ cups chopped walnuts
Evaporated milk

Cream shortening and sugar together. Add eggs one at a time and mix well. Add molasses and water and vanilla. Sift together spices, salt, soda, and flour, and mix with first mixture. Add fruit and nuts. Roll out into rolls 1 inch wide and as long as a cooky sheet, place on greased cooky sheet, and pat down flat. Brush top with evaporated milk and bake 20 minutes in moderate oven (350°). While still warm, cut diagonally into pieces about 1 inch wide. Makes about 16 dozen cookies.

⚒ Consensus Mincemeat ⚒

"Knowledge that venison neck is usually unappreciated, plus past experience that end results make fine gifts for people who have everything else, plus some weather right now so warm it is preferable to sit inside and write rather than go outside and melt, brings you this recipe for Consensus Mincemeat," reports J. S. Barrish.

One venison neck makes a whole lot of mincemeat. But the recipe is being passed on as is—substitute beef if you don't have venison—because it just plain makes good mincemeat. It's moist, meaty, hearty but not too heavy, studded with fruits, rich but not overly sweet.

If you want only 4 to 5 quarts mincemeat, you can reduce each ingredient to approximately one-fifth the amount shown here. However, this does make a good gift item to produce on a large scale, especially, as Mr. Barrish says, "if you give some to the poor fellow who worked so hard to get the deer."

1 venison neck (approximately 10 pounds)
3 tablespoons salt
½ teaspoon white pepper
1 cup cider vinegar
5 pounds beef suet
20 pounds green apples
1 gallon apple cider
7 pounds white sugar
3 pounds brown sugar
1 quart molasses
3 pounds mixed, diced candied fruit
4 tablespoons ground cinnamon
1 tablespoon mace
2 tablespoons ground cloves
4 fresh nutmegs, grated
1 tablespoon ground allspice
10 pounds seeded or seedless raisins
5 pounds currants (dried)
1 fifth brandy
1 fifth rum

Besides these 20 (count them) ingredients, it is necessary to have one very large cooking vessel, as the recipe yields some 6 gallons or more, depending on how big the bones in the neck and how thin the peelings of the apples.

First, wipe all hair off venison neck with damp cloth, or wash the neck if necessary. Place it in pot with just enough water to cover. Add salt, pepper, and vinegar. Bring to boil and continue cooking over low heat until the meat is very tender.

Meanwhile, spend the next two hours or so stripping and discarding membrane from suet; peeling, coring, and mincing apples; then finally assembling all other ingredients.

Remove venison neck from liquid. Save liquid. Separate meat from bones, sinews, and veins. Save all these for the dog. Add suet and apples to liquid (you should have about 2½ to 3 quarts of it) and cook about 20 minutes. Meanwhile mince the meat.

Add to the pot: minced meat, ½ gallon cider, white and brown sugar, molasses, candied fruit, all the spices, remaining ½ gallon cider. Stir and add raisins and currants. Cook until suet is transparent and raisins are plump, stirring to prevent sticking. Between stirrings, sterilize 24 to 30 one-quart Mason jars.

Arrange jars and lids for quick and convenient filling and sealing. Open brandy and set aside near a 1-ounce measure. Open rum and pour into the mincemeat, stirring it vigorously and thoroughly.

Fill first jar to within 1 inch of top, add 1 ounce of brandy, and seal quickly. Repeat until about the twentieth jar. Now you're about to find out whether bones in the neck were too small or apple peel was too thin.

If everything works out properly, the twenty-fourth jar will finish the mincemeat and the brandy.

If not, it must be conceded that another half pint of brandy will be required—and the recipe should have called for a full quart in the first place.

Place jars in as cool and dark a place as you can provide to ripen for at least three weeks. One quart makes two pies. Mincemeat will keep indefinitely.

⚒ Rum and Maple Pecan Pie ⚒

Robert L. Wood submits "an original pie creation inspired by an advertisement for tobacco flavored with rum and maple.

"Some might prefer to pre-cook the filling in a double boiler on top of the stove, but the flavor would be somewhat different; pre-cooking in the oven gives the same conditions as if the pie were baking in the shell all that time." You might also prefer your own favorite pie crust, in which case you should substitute 1 tablespoon lemon juice for water; the sourness of the crust will offset the richness of the filling.

RICH BUTTER PASTRY

2½ cups sifted flour
½ teaspoon salt
1 teaspoon baking powder
1 tablespoon sugar
½ cup plus 2 tablespoons lard or shortening
2 tablespoons butter
1 egg yolk, slightly beaten
1 tablespoon lemon or lime juice
Water

FILLING

3 eggs, beaten
¾ cup light corn syrup
¼ cup (½ cube) melted butter
¾ cup sugar
½ cup maple-flavored syrup
1 tablespoon flour
Pinch of salt
Few drops yellow food coloring
1 cup shelled pecans
¾ teaspoon rum or rum flavoring to taste
1 or 2 drops almond extract (optional)

To make pastry, sift together dry ingredients. Cut in lard and butter until largest pieces are the size of peas. Put egg yolk and lemon juice in glass measuring cup and add enough water to make ½ cup total liquid. Blend with flour mixture. Turn dough onto a floured board and roll to fit a 9 or 10-inch pie pan.

To make filling, mix together all ingredients for filling; place in saucepan and pre-cook in a moderate oven (350°) for about 20 minutes. Then pour into unbaked pie shell (use cooking glove and be careful not to burn yourself). Bake in a moderate oven (350°) an additional 40 to 45 minutes. Makes 8 to 10 servings.

INDEX

A

Alcorn, Richard C., 59, 61
Allin, Col. Benjamin C., III, 84
Appetizers, 122-133. Brussels Sprouts and Double-T Sauce, 129; Caviar Pie, 126. *Cheese:* Roquefort-Cognac Crisps, 132; sandwiches, Post-Poker Platter, 128; Succulent Balls, 131. Definition, 130; fish, Lime-"Cooked," 133; Gizzard Delights, 127; meat, Succulent Subrics, 124; meatballs, Spicy, 130. *Mushrooms:* Earthy, 125; Happy Hour, 123; Wine Appeteasers, 131. *Oysters:* Parmesan, 132; Rock Salt, 123. Piroshki, Chicken Liver, 124; pizza, Mexican, Pobrecito, 126; Sardine, Tangy dip, 129; Shrimp Beau Brummell, 125; zucchini, Flower Fritters, 128
Auerbach, Herbert, 107
Avocado. With eggs, Mexican style, 77; and rockfish, 61; salad dressing, 104; in salads, 101, 102, 104, 107, 109
Ax, John, 135

B

Baked Dishes. Bananas, 92; bean casserole, 88. *Cheese:* enchiladas, 83; Swiss pie, 79. *Chicken:* in gin, 39; with herbs, 40; lasagne, cheese casserole, 48; livers, 52; thighs with liver stuffing and soy marinade, 50. Chiles rellenos, 81; corn on the cob, 99; *Crab:* asparagus, spaghetti casserole, 63; rice, cheese casserole, 64; shrimp, cheese casserole, 67. Dove and grapes in wine, 56; ham with bananas, 25; kidney beans, 87. *Lamb:* neck in wine and herbs, 23; tongue with vegetables, 32. Mushrooms and oysters, 93; oysters in cream, 71; pheasant in wine, mushroom sauce, 57; pizza flavored pie, 75. *Pork:* chops in wine, 24; sandwich, 115. Potatoes, stuffed, 86; rabbit in wine, 15. *Rice:* with

clams, 84; in wine, 84. Rockfish fillet and capers in foil, 61; sandwich, Mexican, 116; sole fillet with shrimp stuffing and egg sauce, 62; spareribs in brown sugar, 26; sweetbreads with Supreme Sauce, 33; turkey, spinach casserole, 51; turnips with cracker topping, 99; veal chops with cheese, 35
Barnette, Col. E. Jeff, 64, 92, 131
Barrish, J. S., 156
Beans. Garbanzo, kidney, blackeyed peas casserole, 88; kidney bake, 87; with lamb, 20; pink, 89; soup, 146
Beckett, Robert E., 92
Beef. Corned, Authoritative, 17. *Ground:* for cabbage rolls, 95; chuck, for bean simmer, 89; chuck, sandwich, 114; meatballs, Freshly minted, 19; Oriental style, with Eye Appeal, 17; with rice, Turkish Exotique, 18; with Roquefort, Hamburgers a la Phoops, 19. Hash, The World's Best, 140; kidneys, *see* Variety Cuts; liver, *see* Variety Cuts; rump roast cooked in wine and herbs, Lazy Man's Roast, 10. Short ribs, Sweet and Sour, 9. *Stew:* Mexican style, Tortilla Flats, 11; S.O.B., 144; oxtail, Hangover, 143. *Veal:* in bean casserole, 88; chops, Francaise, 35; scallopini A.R.P.A., 21; stew, 145
Beef Steak. *Chuck:* Beergers, 14; Burgundy, 14. Flank, The Flavor of Green Chiles, 16. *Round:* Ground Oriental, 12; Wined and Onions, 35. *Sirloin:* in Burgundy, Norwegian Meatballs, 31; Chow Vegetables, 8; with herbs and wine, Siciliano Broil, 9; in Kahlua, American Special-Western Style, 8; top, Oriental style, Korean Broil, 10
Beer. With beefsteak, 14; stew, 143, 145
Bergeson, William Talbot, 81
Berlowitz, Laurence, 60
Bialiej, Bixele, 28, 125
Blacklidge, F. E., 17, 112
Blair, Bob, 140
Blanchfield, Jim, 80

Blohm, Clyde L., 12
Bock, Charles, 73
Boiled Dishes. Chicken with dumplings, 38; pork butt with cabbage, 28
Borscht, *see* soup
Bradbury, John, 18
Bread, 111-121. Bagels, Co-existence Water, 113. *Blintzes:* Mexican style, con Queso, 117; with mushrooms, 121. Cornmeal, Mexican Spoon, 112; muffins, bran, with Crunch, 112; Orange-Raisin, 120; pizza, Yankee, 117; sandwich, Mexican, Tacos de Aguacate, 116
Brinck, Chester G., 54
Broiled Dishes. Abalone patties, 66; chicken with lime-dill flavor, 42; ground beef with Roquefort, 19; lamb patties, 20; sirloin in wine and herbs, 9; sole fillet with mushroom sauce, 59
Brown, Frank R., 71, 91
Bryan, Lloyd, 23
Burke, John S., 108, 109

C

Cake. Coffee, California, 118; Fruit-Full, 153; Pineapple-Cheese Pudding, 149
Calhoun, Gen. F.E., 99
Capers. With fruit salad, 102; with rockfish fillets, 61; in salad dressing, 106
Casserole Dishes. Bean bake, 88; chicken, lasagne, cheese bake, 67. *Crab:* shrimp, cheese bake, 67; spaghetti, asparagus bake, 63. Onion, French, 135
Caviar, appetizer, 126
Chalk, Earl, 75
Cheese, 74-84. Appetizers, 128, 131, 132. Blue, in salad, 107. *Cheddar:* chiles Rellenos, 81; in cornmeal bread, 112; in eggplant fry, 94; Enchiladas de Arroz y Queso, 83; Roman Cheese Pie, 75. *Cottage:* with green salad, 101; in salad dressing, 108. In crab, shrimp casserole, 67. *Jack:* Chiles Rellenos Digresion, 81; with eggs, Mexican style, 77. Lasagne, Four-Cheese, 78;

Longhorn, Enchiladas de Arroz y Queso, 83; Mozarella, sardine sandwich, 116. *Roquefort:* with beef patties, 19; dressing, 107; in salad, 105. Swiss pie, Tyrol Tarts, 79
Cherry, Alfred, 79, 151
Chiles. With beef steak, 16; with eggs, 77; in enchiladas, 83; rellenos, 81; with steamed rice, 81
Chittock, Robert, 48
Chowder, *see* Soup
Clamp, A. E., 132
Coffman, Rawlins, 44
Colby, E., 27, 42, 65, 110
Colombe, Paul de Sainte, 35
Conrow, Thomas, M., 76, 110
Cookies. Chewy Fruit Bar, 155; Oatmeal Fruit, 151
Cooper, Ted L., 116
Corn. On the Cob, 94, 99; creamed, in cornmeal bread, 112
Costa, Mike, 72
Cota, Dan., 90
Crab, *see* Shellfish
Crockett, Charles C., 52
Cronemiller, F. P., 11, 143, 144

D

Damon, Noel E., 36
Delkin, Fred L., Jr., 136
Destin, Vic, 107
Desserts, 147-156. Cake, 118, 149, 153; cookies, 151, 155; fruit, 148, 149, 150, 151, 152; fruit cake, 153; mincemeat, 156; mousse, 154; pie, 152, 157; pudding, 155; pudding sauce, 148, 154; sherbet, 151; zabaglione, 150
Dressing. Avocado, Simplicity, 105; Caesar, 101; Chutney Caper, 106; citrus, Orange-Tomato, 109; cottage cheese, Gourmet for Fatties, 108; honey-vinegar, 102; Leeky Lemon, 108; Louis, 104; mayonnaise, for prawns, 109; Roquefort, Short-Time, 107; vinegar, for cucumbers, 103
Dumplings, with boiled chicken, 38
Dutch Oven Dishes. Beef short ribs, 9; onions, steam stuffed, 98
Dyar, Dr. Robert, 63